FROM
WORRY
TO
WEALTH

FROM
WORRY
TO
WEALTH

A Step-by-Step Guide to
Achieving Financial Success

Ben Lyons

Copyright © 2021 by Benjamin Lyons

All rights reserved. This book or any portion of thereof may not be reproduced or used in any manner whatsoever without the express written permission of the author except for the use of brief quotations in a book review.

ISBN-13: 9798519096355

Editing and Layout by Rachel Greene for elfinpen designs
Additional Editing by Gabe Bustos from Money Club
Self-Assessment Tools by Josh Massey from Money Club

www.wearemoneyclub.com

CONTENTS

Foreword: Aaron Velky i
Introduction 1
ONE: Anyone Can Become Wealthy 9
TWO: My Story 29
THREE: The Wealth Creation Formula 47
   Case Study #1 .... *59*
FOUR: Assessing Your Financial Self 67
   Case Study #2 .... *89*
FIVE: Step 1: Leave Worry Behind 95
   Case Study #3. .... *121*
SIX: Step 2: Generate Investable Income 127
   Case Study #4 .... *149*
SEVEN: Step 3: Discover Your Asset Strategy ... 155
   Case Study #5 .... *185*
EIGHT: The Power of Leverage 191
   Case Study #6 .... *205*
NINE: The Role of Time 211
   Case Study #7 .... *221*
TEN: From Worry to Wealth 227

FOREWORD

By Aaron Velky

It was May 10th, 2017. I was sitting in a coffee shop that's known for the bustling noise of business meetings and the clanking of breakfast dishes. I was excited to meet Ben Lyons. We entrepreneurs believe that every meeting could be the opening of a new life, whereby the individual in front of us would change and shape our lives for the better.

Introduced by a school headmaster, we both had a passion for teaching others about money. I was sure I could win Ben over and enlist him on the mission I had burning inside me that we had begun to build at Money Club. Little did I know that Ben would be enrolling me as his student that day, and that meeting him would dramatically change my life and my company.

My work and passions have taken me all over the world and through many different industries. I am the CEO and Co-Founder of Money Club, a financial intelligence training company; an executive and lifestyle coach; and an author.

My primary driver for success, especially early on, was the idea of escaping the need to work. Wealth, it seemed, was my best way out of the rat race that was grinding me and so many of my peers down.

But in my head, I was waiting for a golden ticket. That single moment that would check the box and allow me to pop the champagne, throw a party, and never have to work again. One 9-figure transfer to the bank, and I'd never have to worry again, right?

Like many, I dove in head first, without much of a plan. Over the years since quitting my day job, I've been able to build Money Club into a reputable brand with the help of my co-founder and team, creating a business that has shared financial intelligence lessons with thousands of young adults and hundreds more adults. Learning about money, how to make it and how to grow it, was a passion that we turned into a business. But something was amiss as I started to grow and have higher-level conversations with more adults—some that were already financially successful and others that were still figuring it out.

I was beginning to feel like a fraud.

If I wasn't already wealthy and did not know everything about building wealth, how would I guide others? Who would help us guide our intermediate students to the next level? Hell—who would guide us, the team, so that we could guide others?

At the time, I had a vision of an organization that could transcend teaching kids and teach adults as well, but I didn't know what I didn't know. Specifically, I didn't know how to do what I saw in my head. I was driven by scarcity and making decisions based on fear—I was treading water. I was worried!

Discussions internally at Money Club led us to believe we could grow as a venture-backed, purpose-driven organization, combining the consciousness of social ventures with the capacity and acceleration that profit provided. We felt that other financial education efforts lacked innovation, required refreshing and modernization, and needed our voices.

But we didn't know how to get there.

Over the next eighteen months, Ben joined the team at Money Club and helped us sketch and design how our new alignment would work, carefully crafting the future of an organization designed to disrupt. Ben's commitment to support us was as resolute as his insistence on challenging and testing us, especially me as the leader.

In the last four years Ben has taught us the principles that you'll find in this book. We learned about leverage, about delivering value, and about building education that took our behavioral methods and merged it with proven, high-level tactics. With his experience, wisdom, and network, we reimagined Money Club. Ben installed in us a new driving force.

In many ways, we were able to build upon the foundations of what we knew best—the social-emotional components of people and money, how to teach in fun and engaging ways, and the fundamentals of finance—and combine it with Ben's amazing understanding of business, income, assets, leverage, time, and wealth generation. Our training and educational content improved to new levels. Our business strategies and capacity to help people was extended.

Personally, the lessons I have learned from Ben go well beyond anything I learned in college as a financial economics major. I have learned to shift my mindset from one of worry and scarcity to one of wealth and abundance. I have increased my specialized knowledge and am continuing to become the leader I knew was within me. That inner leader just needed the guidance of someone who had accomplished the level of success I was striving for—capable of building wealth that at first felt so far away and impossible because of my history and background.

I used to believe that one day I'd have money "figured out." That I would wake up a better business leader, entrepreneur, and writer. I believed that I could eliminate worry and fear without being surrounded by the right leaders and coaches. But now, having spent over six figures getting coaching on my mindset, skills and leadership, I realized something very special, something that we're all very excited to share with you in this book:

The movement from worry to wealth begins with a decision to alter your mindset, followed by the first investment in your education; from there, the limits are only determined by you.

As you read this book, you may find yourself asking different questions, wanting different answers, or challenging the things you hear friends and family say—the things they've told you for years that you took as truth.

The strategies in this book will help you the same way they've helped me, if you apply them. They showed me what was possible and helped me understand the path that was ahead of me. I had to realize that it wasn't a single choice that I was making. I was committing to a long-term plan with a teacher like Ben Lyons—someone that could help me as long as I put in the work to continue to learn and grow.

This book will guide you down a new path that will change your future, if you allow it. This is the beginning of the journey for you, but it's also the beginning of *our* journey beside you. Together, Ben Lyons and Money Club are here to walk with you, hand in hand. We're here to make you successful.

You'll learn the wealth formula and all practical applications of its principles. You'll have access to a variety of tools that have been produced by Money Club, and you'll get to hear all the tales of the success and lessons that come directly from Ben. We'll provide you with tools, insights, education, and a support network to help you along your journey, which you'll chart for yourself throughout the book.

I wanted more out of life, but I didn't know how to get there. And since that fateful day in May of 2017, I've listened, trusted, and leaned on Ben as a source of inspiration, direction, and education.

And he's never taught me wrong.

Welcome to *From Worry to Wealth*, a collaborative writing effort led by Ben Lyons, supported by the team at Money Club.

If Ben's education does for you even a single percentage of what it did for me, this book will create an entirely new life for you.

Aaron Velky
CEO, Money Club

INTRODUCTION

What do you think of when you hear the word "wealth"?

Is it a bank account with seven figures? Is it owning an upscale house or driving a top-of-the-line car? Maybe you think of fame and fortune, and several celebrities come to mind. What about Jeff Bezos, Bill Gates, Barack Obama, Donald Trump, or Kim Kardashian? How do we define wealth?

No matter what your picture of wealth is, I imagine that many of you reading this book don't consider yourselves "wealthy." Instead, you probably picked up this book because you feel more "worried" than wealthy.

Most people are worried about money, at one level or another. Some of you are worried about having enough to retire or send your kids to college. Some of you are worried about the fate of your job or the stability of the economy.

Some of you are worried you won't make it to the end of the month—or, perhaps, the end of the week.

No matter what your current financial situation is, I'm here to tell you that it doesn't have to be this way. No matter what you do for a living, and no matter what your income level is, you possess the ability to build wealth for you and your family, and you can do it starting today.

Normally, when I teach about financial success and make the audacious claim above, I get one of two responses. The first is the objection that **"Money isn't everything. Being wealthy isn't the most important aspect of my life."**

My response is: You're right! Money isn't *the* most important thing, but it is *an* important thing. I believe that our lives are comprised of five spheres, or "selves":

- Physical self
- Spiritual self
- Psychological self
- Social self
- Financial self

Our "selves" are like the organs in our body. They are interdependent. Neither is more important than the other, but they all affect the entire system. When one organ is sick, the whole body is affected. On the other hand, if any organ is thriving and healthy, the rest of the body benefits.

The same is true of our financial selves. While the financial self does not outweigh any of our other selves, its health critically affects our overall well-being. If we are not doing well financially, it is almost guaranteed that we are suffering in other areas. Conversely, if our financial self is well, it can help inspire growth throughout our whole being. This is why it is imperative to take the health of our financial self seriously. It's my goal through this book to show you how to improve your financial self without sacrificing any of your other beings in the process.

The next response I get to my proposition about wealth building is usually simply **"I can't,"** or **"Wealth isn't for me."** As a financial advisor, investor, and business owner with over 35 years of experience, I have heard this phrase more times than I can count. So many people I encounter—even those that are coming to me for financial advice—have preemptively discounted themselves from becoming wealthy. They're convinced wealth building is beyond their reach, usually for one of the following reasons:

- I don't make enough money.
- I don't have enough time in the day with all of my other obligations.

- I don't want to deal with real estate or stocks.
- I spend too much time worrying about how to make rent; I don't have any energy to worry about investing.
- I already have a 401k through my job; that's all I need to retire.
- The system makes it impossible for me to build wealth.
- I have too much credit card debt.
- Most people who are rich have had it handed to them through a lucky opportunity or inheritance.

Believe it or not, none of these could be further from the truth! A quick look at statistics shows us that there is a vast amount of wealth available in the United States[1]. Opportunity is not evenly distributed, but compared to most other countries in the world, opportunity in America *is* more available to everyone.

There are abundant resources that are accessible to everyone, and you don't have to be an investment banker or stock broker to take advantage of them. You don't have to strike it lucky with a new invention or a prime business deal, and you definitely don't have to win the lottery. In fact, you might be earning all the money you need at your current job

---

[1] https://www.investopedia.com/insights/worlds-top-economies/

to enable you to build net worth, secure your and your children's future, and retire comfortably.

You can do this because wealth isn't based on lucky circumstances or limited to certain professions. Instead, wealth is built from four core ingredients that combine to produce a sustainable flow of money. These four key components to wealth building are:

Income, Assets, Leverage, and Time

These four ingredients act like a "recipe" that can work for anyone at any time. Just like most cake recipes call for some combination of flour, sugar, eggs, and oil, most successful formulas for wealth utilize a combination of income, assets, leverage, and time. Some people might use more flour and sugar and make a pound cake, while others might use copious amounts of egg and make an angel food cake. Some people will want chocolate, some vanilla, and some a swirl of both. But even though the ratio of ingredients might be different, giving the final product a different "flavor," everyone still uses the same basic ingredients to produce the same basic result: an edible cake.

Another way to look at wealth building is to imagine each ingredient as a variable in a math equation with an infinite number of solutions. 2+2+2+2 equals eight, but so does 4+2+1+1 or even 8+0+0+0. In the same way, each individual can use a different combination of the variables in the wealth formula, tailored to their unique circumstances and abilities, to get the same result: stable, self-generating wealth.

My goal with this book is to debunk the myth that wealth is inaccessible. I want to explain the wealth creation formula to you and walk you through each variable, showing you how each can be applied to your financial self regardless of your individual circumstances. I'll share my personal journey with you, and then I'll help you take a complete assessment of your financial situation. Then, based on where you're currently at and your unique skills and interests, I'll guide you through the process of creating a realistic, actionable plan to build a strong financial self for you and your family.

Wealth is available to everyone. I will show you that anyone—even someone working a low-wage job—can take control of their financial life and make their money work for them. By understanding the components of wealth creation and applying them to your unique circumstances, you can build your own future, starting today.

People do not prioritize financial literacy, but they are putting their lives on the line without it.

ONE

Anyone Can Become Wealthy

I've just made a pretty audacious claim: **Anyone, even someone working a low-wage job, can become wealthy.**

If that's true, the logical question then becomes: Why *isn't* everyone wealthy? All it takes is a quick glance around your neighborhood to realize that the average American family is "just making it"—or worse. If wealth isn't solely dependent on your salary, and you don't need lucky circumstances to attain it, then why aren't more people financially successful?

The many complicated answers to this question fall into two large buckets: socio-political answers and personal agency answers.

By socio-political, I am referring to hundreds of years of political, cultural, and societal influences that have created large inequities along the many different intersecting spheres of how we interact with each other as human beings: class, race, geography, gender, etc. None of these are a reflection on someone's inherent abilities, but they do greatly affect the environment in which we can grow our abilities. As entrepreneur and CEO Leilah Janah says, "Talent is equally distributed, but opportunity is not."

On the other hand, we must consider personal agency. We are free and independent beings, and our self-will and capability of choice play a huge role in our own fate. We can set our own goals, values, and ambitions, and in every situation we encounter, we can choose to respond in such a way that either takes us one step closer to those goals or one step further away. Every day, we can choose how we spend our time, money, energy, and attention. It may not feel this way in the moment, and the uphill climb often seems very steep, but success is the culmination of thousands of small decisions. With one small step at a time, you can climb a mountain.

It is certainly true that these two buckets—socio-political and personal agency—are largely interwoven. Our attitudes, behaviors, education, and connections are all influenced by the environment in which we grew up, but it is not within the scope of this book to discuss the social, political, and cultural reasons why some people aren't wealthy. These are very challenging and important issues that need to be addressed by each and every one of us, but they are not issues I am qualified to address here.

I can, however, talk about personal agency. I firmly believe that whether we are 20 or 60 years old, we maintain the right to choose how we respond to each day of our lives. That right to choose is what we will address in this book, but in order to do so, we first need to become self-aware of *how* we became the person we are today. That self-awareness will give us invaluable insight into how we can improve the person we will be tomorrow.

The Happiness of Wealth

First, we need to answer a very important question: *Why* do we want to become wealthy? If you picked up this book, I can assume that you'd like to be wealthy, at least in theory. But why? Why is wealth something we should pursue?

Everyone has a unique—and probably very complicated—answer as to why they want to become wealthy. I personally have a very simple explanation for why people should become wealthy. I'm going to make another audacious claim and say that **you should become wealthy because wealth will enable you to pursue happiness.**

That may sound scandalous to some, but let me elaborate. Ask yourself: What, really, *is* wealth? Technically speaking, wealth is the accumulation of money. When many people think of wealth, they imagine millionaires from old monied families, which is an example of *generational wealth*, or money that is passed on from generation to generation. Other people imagine the physical representations of wealth—the cars, houses, bank accounts, and real estate properties that money can buy.

But the word wealth has come to mean much more in our modern society. To most people, "wealth" is a measure of our ability to buy expensive things. It also enables us to afford expensive activities, like taking nice vacations or sending our kids to private schools. For many, the freedom to buy these things is equated with happiness. But does that mean wealth will really make us happy?

Frankly, it depends. It depends on how you use money, and it depends on whether or not your financial decisions align with what is truly best for you and your family.

I love the way Money Club defines money values for their students: **Being wealthy is making enough money to live a life that is fulfilling to *you*.** Not to the standards of self-worth by which society measures you, but to *your* standards.

The concept of having enough, doing enough, or being enough is very different for every person, and success requires work in each of our different selves—social, emotional, physical, and spiritual. But how much time we are able to invest in those different selves is directly tied to how much time we need to spend earning money to sustain our lifestyle. In other words, our happiness is more a reflection of how we are spending our *time* than how we are spending our money.

Here's a simple example. Say you're a parent and your greatest joy would be to spend the weekends with your kids, taking them on trips to parks, the zoo, and their grandparents' house. However, if you have to work every weekend to pay rent, no amount of money will make you happy if it distracts you from time with your kids. A new car or a better house isn't going to create lasting happiness for you. Instead, your goal should be to get into a position where you didn't have to work weekends. Money would enable you to do that, but your newfound joy wouldn't come from your large bank account or improved job: It would come from the freedom to invest your time and energy in the things that matter most to you, your kids. In other words, **money unlocks the ability to spend our time and energy on the things we enjoy.**

This is not to say that having nice possessions is inherently bad. Each of us gets to choose the lifestyle we want. But a problem arises when we are spending in excess on objects not because we actually want them, but because we *think* we want them—because our circles of influence and society at large have convinced us that we want them.

We all know that spending money on a drug habit to fill a deeper hole in one's social or emotional health is not a good use of money. But swap out "drug habit" with "expensive cars," "fancy clothes," or "5-star hotels" and the sentence is just as true. We often try to use money to directly fill holes that we have in our other selves, but money can't always do that. Time, however, can.

Whatever your goals are in life, money can help you reach them, because money can buy you time. Whether you want to raise a family of five in the suburbs, build a homestead and live off the land, or work remotely from a different country each year, money is absolutely essential in helping you reach those goals.

This is why it's important not to equate wealth with a certain lifestyle, a particular house or car, or a specific career and income level. Becoming wealthy isn't about adding more to your life. It's about removing the things that are eating at your time: a meaningless job you hate, an unhealthy relationship you're dependent on, or the crippling stress of financial instability.

We'll talk more about the proper utilization of time in a later chapter, but for now, understand that my goal with this book is not to push you into living a particular lifestyle or affording a certain type of car or house. My goal with this book is to teach you the principles of financial success so that you can spend your time, energy, and money in such a way that reduces stress and worry in your life and enables you to pursue what you find truly fulfilling. I want you to be happy *and* wealthy, and I believe you can achieve both, no matter what your current situation is.

A Map of You

There are many financial advice books that will do a great job of inspiring you to pursue your dream career. There are many books that will teach invaluable lessons about managing your personal finances, cutting back your spending, or having healthy money conversations with your spouse. There are also many books that will help you succeed in a particular business or investment strategy.

While we might address some of the topics above, this book isn't any of those things. This book isn't just about theories and concepts; it's a guided tour to help you effectively and sustainably apply those theories and concepts to your own unique situation. The goal of this book is not just to help you understand that there is a sustainable path to long-term wealth generation, but also to give you the tools, awareness, and support to help you find yours. By discovering your own personal strategies to solve the four variables of the wealth formula—investable income, acquiring assets, leverage, and time—you will unlock the power to follow the path to wealth with confidence. You need a roadmap to wealth, but not a generic "one size fits all" one. You need a map of *you*.

To do this, we're going to spend a great deal of time assessing and understanding our own unique financial situation. This involves more than just tallying our bank accounts and credit card debts; as I mentioned in the beginning of this chapter, we need to truly understand not only ourselves but also how we got here. That's why I've partnered with Money Club to build videos and interactive tools to help you self-assess both where you are right now and what steps you need to take to most effectively reach your destination.

Included with this book is free access to online videos and tools to help you assess and track your finances along your journey. These tools will help you understand your strengths and weaknesses with regards to your finances, career, and long-term goals. Whether it's the Money Personality Quiz (where you'll uncover your natural tendencies with money) or the Your Way to 20k income self-assessment (where you'll discover your most effective strategies to earn more income and build asset value), these tools will give you the self-awareness you need to plan your most effective strategies to improve your habits, earn more income, build asset value, and generate wealth.

Think of this book and the accompanying online materials as a "field guide" to your own financial self-discovery. To access the online tools, visit **Wealthtools.WorrytoWealthBook.com**. In Chapter 4, we'll explain how each online resource works and when to use it during your financial journey.

If you are asking yourself if it's really necessary that you take *yet another* online quiz, I must stress that the answer is **yes**. Whether you take the time to use each tool as you work through the book or go back after you finish reading and do them all at once, you *must* use them if you want to make these principles work for you. You can't design a personalized plan if you aren't intimately familiar with yourself and your circumstances. Throughout the book I'll be limited to general examples; there's no way I can accurately address everyone and every situation. I can demonstrate that the formula will work for everyone, but only you can put in the effort to make it effective for you.

The Keys to the Kingdom

In 2019, the United States was home to 40% percent of the world's total millionaires[2]. In fact, over 675,000 adults in the U.S. became millionaires for the first time that year, meaning that on average, over 1,800 people became millionaires every day[3].

It's true that there are very important socio-political problems to solve in this country, all of which affect people's pursuit of wealth. But compared to other places around the world, the United States still possesses tremendous opportunity that is, in general, accessible to anyone willing to work hard and smart enough. It is all too easy to use our socio-political landscape as an excuse to avoid that hard work and investment. If we tell ourselves it's impossible for us to build wealth, we won't try, and our prophecy will become self-fulfilling. That's why it does us no good to view ourselves as a victim of forces that are out of our control. It is true that we can't control everything, but we can control how we respond to the cards we are dealt, and that is where we should focus our energy.

---

[2] https://www.statista.com/statistics/268411/countries-with-the-most-millionaires/

[3] https://markets.businessinsider.com/news/stocks/10-countries-that-minted-the-most-new-millionaires-in-2019-2019-10-1028620898

This is why I firmly believe that **our attitude about money is the most important factor in determining financial success.** Attitude underlies everything. Our financial behaviors stem from our mindset, values, and beliefs about money. Here are some easy examples: Someone who was raised to believe that money is evil might never ask for a raise or promotion. Someone who was raised to believe that we need expensive things to keep up with our peers might never develop the investable income needed to grow wealth. Attitude defines our motivations, for good or bad, and our motivations determine where we will ultimately end up in life.

To begin to understand your attitudes about wealth, consider your upbringing and ask yourself: What kind of attitudes did your parents have about money? Your parents were likely your first financial "influencers," but they were hardly the only ones. Some other people who have had a say in your financial development might include:

- Teachers
- Peers
- Religious figures
- Sports stars and celebrities
- Social media influencers
- Mentors
- Employers

- Spouses and other family members

And the list goes on. All of these people have shaped who you are and how you think about money, often in subconscious ways. This is why I strongly encourage you to evaluate your relationships and ask yourself who is influencing your financial decisions, both past and present. This is not about shifting blame, however. We examine our past so we can better understand ourselves, but we must remember that we are not bound to our influencers. They do not control us or who we become. At the end of the day, our attitudes and responses are determined by us, and only us.

This is why I say that attitude can be entirely self-taught. No matter how you were raised or what influences you encountered growing up, you possess the ability to determine who you are going to be and how you are going to react. You can teach yourself to build discipline, to take healthy risks, and to believe the truth about money and wealth building. Every day, you can *become* a new person.

Becoming a new person requires that you learn and grow, which is why I believe **the second most important factor to financial success is education.** By education, I don't just mean a college degree. College degrees can be useful, but they are not required for building wealth. The internet is full of stories of now-multimillionaires that dropped out of college: Bill

Gates, Steven Spielberg, Mark Zuckerberg, and Steve Jobs. (As you'll find out in the next chapter, I didn't go to college at all.)

The reason many people falsely assume a college education is required for wealth building is that people with college degrees often hold higher-paying jobs, but income is not the sole determinant of wealth. Someone who makes $100k a year but owes $500k on their house, cars, and credit cards would have a lower net worth than someone who makes $20k a year but has no debt. In fact, many people with high incomes find themselves in deep financial trouble because they do not know how to manage those paychecks. I have worked with hundreds of people who have more letters after their name than in it and yet have almost no financial skills.

When I say "education," I mean "financial intelligence." Simply put, if you understand how money works and how to manage it, you can control it and multiply it. If you do not understand how money works and how to manage it, it will control you, and you will lose and waste it instead of building it.

Thankfully for us, financial education doesn't have to occur in a classroom—and frankly, in most schools across the country, it isn't. The majority of schools, including institutes of higher education, do not emphasize financial literacy, even at a basic level. We've all jokingly complained on social media that we got out of high school without knowing how to do our taxes, but this points to a systemic problem in the American education system. I saw it on full display when I guided my four children through private high schools and colleges. The problem is only exaggerated in college; as we just mentioned, someone can emerge from 7+ years of college knowing actual rocket science and still not have any idea what to do with their paycheck.

This is one reason I believe many Americans have low net worth and fail to move themselves up the wealth scale for generation after generation. Our education system is not designed to teach wealth. And even when there is financial education, often the people who are teaching the principles of wealth creation have not created wealth for themselves, with few exceptions. Would you hire someone who is not physically fit to be your personal trainer? Would you learn baseball from someone who has never played professionally and can't even hit a pitch themselves? Of course not. And yet we routinely invite non-wealthy people to teach us about money.

However, we can combat this while spending little to no money. We can learn everything we need about finances from books, podcasts, lectures, and other online resources. The library and YouTube have more than enough to get most people on the path to wealth. But *you* know that, because you've already started teaching yourself. By reading this book, you've begun your own financial self-education.

That, truly, is the only thing hindering most people from becoming wealthy: the knowledge of what steps *they*, in their unique situation, need to take to become wealthy. With knowledge comes confidence, and with confidence comes action.

Confidence is the belief that your actions will produce an intended outcome. Many people fail financially because they do not truly believe their actions will produce a positive financial outcome over time. They don't believe that a certain savings plan, budget, or job change will truly bring the results they dream about. Worse, they don't believe the results they dream about are even possible. This leads to inaction and ineffectiveness.

Let's go back to the cake analogy we introduced at the beginning of the book. When you bake a cake, you follow the recipe because you're confident it will produce an edible product. If you didn't confidently know that mixing flour, sugar, eggs, and oil and baking it at a certain temperature for a certain time would produce a cake, would you do it? Of course not! But because you *know* you're going to get a delicious cake if you follow the recipe, you do it, and you carefully follow all of the steps in order.

That is why attitude and education are the two most important keys in your wealth journey, and why they are the two most important concepts I want to teach you in this book. You need to truly *believe* that wealth is possible for you, and you need to know and understand the "recipe" that will get you there.

To that end, we'll spend the remainder of the book demystifying the core components of wealth creation, showing you how to assess your current financial situation, and helping you build a multi-stage plan to grow your net worth.

Actually *implementing* that plan will require a lot of hard work, especially up front. I won't lie to you. It won't be easy, but neither is the stress of working for a company that may lay you off next month. Neither is the anxiety of piling up medical bills or the pain of your children taking on debt because you can't afford to help them with their education.

You can avoid that. You just need to learn how.

Growing up, my parents struggled very badly with money and fought horribly over it. It created a tremendous amount of stress and insecurity for me. I had never thought of myself as capable or deserving of wealth, because my influencers never gave me any reason to believe that. But one fateful day, three months before my 19th birthday, I met one person at the right time, and it unlocked a burning curiosity in me. I suddenly realized that I needed to understand why my parents were suffering so much financially, and figure out how I could avoid that fate for myself.

That curiosity led to confidence, and by the age of 25, I owned 100 rental properties and a business worth one million dollars. Thirty-seven years later I'm writing to you, hoping to instill in you that same curiosity and confidence to build your best financial self. If you follow the principles and lessons outlined in this book, I have absolutely no doubt that you will climb up the mountain from worry to wealth.

In the internet world, everyone is a mentor and an influencer. Be very careful who is influencing your road map to your best financial self.

TWO

My Story

No matter the subject, I always suggest taking important advice only from someone who has "been there, done that"—not from the person who is filled only with theoretical information. Take advice from someone who has lived through the ups and downs—someone who is well-qualified and has gained first-hand experience in the particular field you want to excel in.

That is why I want to take the time to properly introduce myself. Even though the methods in this book are time-proven, I don't expect you to take my word for it. You deserve to know where I've been and how I got to where I am. I want to show you how I've put these principles into practice in my own life and demonstrate how they worked for me. That involves more than just telling you my annual salary and gross net worth—I want to take you back to the beginning and show you the very simple thing that got me started on my financial journey.

I did not grow up particularly poor or wealthy; we were what most consider solidly middle class. My dad put himself through college by taking night classes over an 11-year period, earning a degree in computer science. My mother did not go to college and worked as an office manager for a physical therapist.

The challenge in our family was that both of my parents had grown up poor. My dad, in particular, had been raised in an orphanage and been dirt poor most of his life. My grandmother was a sex worker and my grandfather died when my dad was only six years old. The insecurity of this extreme poverty was scary and gave my dad a scarcity mindset regarding money. He made it clear repeatedly, while my siblings and I were growing up, that there was very little money for anything.

We lived in a good neighborhood with fairly "typical" middle-class people, but my house was the house that all the neighbors would complain about to their friends and family. I'm sure many of you have a similar house in your neighborhood: cars in the front on cinder blocks, overgrown yard, house never kept up. That was us.

My dad always told me that unless I went to college, I would never get a good job and make money. In his mind, formal education was what got him out of poverty, and therefore, that was the path I had to take.

During high school, I excelled in two areas: physical education and metal shop. Those were the only two classes I got As in because, candidly, they were the only classes I paid any attention to. I had truly little ambition outside of sports and building things with metal. In my head, I never saw myself attending college because I did not see myself as smart or as "a college kid." I did, however, really want to do something in the fitness or exercise business.

When I graduated from high school, I was voted most likely to be a metal shop teacher. I got a combined 520 on my SAT, out of 1,600. I was in the bottom 1%! Coupled with my poor grades in high school, the only college I could get accepted into was community college. So, I filled out paperwork to go to community college the year after I graduated high school. Over that summer, however, something happened that dramatically shifted the trajectory of my life.

My Life-Changing Event

The beginning of my transformation happened when I met a man named Terry Wilson while working nights as a trainer at the Merritt Athletic Club in Woodlawn, Maryland, when I was 18 years old. Terry talked me out of going into the fitness business, and he gave me a book called *Think and Grow Rich* by Napoleon Hill.

At the time, reading was challenging for me, but the book was very interesting, and it made sense even to me. One of the main points Hill made is that, to be successful, you need to pick one *specific* field to study and become an expert in. I immediately decided that I needed to pick a specific path for myself. I made a list of all the possible fields I could think of that I was even remotely interested in. From that list, Terry convinced me that real estate was a very lucrative career.

Unfortunately, I was only 18 years old, and I didn't know anyone in the field except one woman in my neighborhood, who was a realtor. So armed with that mere knowledge, I went up to her house and knocked on the door. When she answered, I declared, "Mrs. Sacki, I understand you are a real estate agent. I was wondering if you have any real estate books I could borrow?"

Mrs. Sacki invited me in and had me wait by the front door. A few minutes later, she came back and handed me two books on real estate, and so I said thank you and left to start reading.

The following Saturday, I was jogging in my parents' neighborhood when this nice Volvo pulled up next to me. The driver rolled down his window, so I stopped jogging and asked if I could help him.

The man asked me if I was Ben, and I replied, "Yeah, why?" He went on to introduce himself as Ron, then asked me if he could speak with me next Saturday at 10am at his house. He handed me a business card with his address on it.

Curious, I asked him what this was about. He responded, "Were you the one at Mrs. Sacki's house last week asking to borrow real estate books?" I nodded. He then told me that his wife had been in Mrs. Sacki's kitchen having tea when I knocked on the door. She came home and told her husband about me, and then Ron came to find me. That was enough explanation for me, so I agreed to meet him.

The following Saturday morning I showed up at his house at 10am sharp. The first thing I noticed was how nice his house was and how beautifully decorated it was. I knocked on the door and a woman answered; she introduced herself to me as Ron's wife and invited me to wait in the living room. Before I could take a seat, Ron walked in, greeted me with a hand-shake, and thanked me for coming.

Our brief conversation went like this:

"Ben, how old are you?"

"I'm 18."

"How would you like to be able to retire by age thirty?"

For a kid who had almost flunked out of high school, this sounded like a dream come true. I immediately responded with, "That would be awesome! What do I need to do?"

Ron went on to explain that he and his father owned a real estate company. His father was up in age and would be retiring soon, and they could use help at the office. At first, this sounded like a great deal. But as Ron went into more detail about his "job offer," the reality wasn't what most people would have called a "good opportunity."

Ron bluntly stated that if I came to work for him for free—yes, free!—he would teach me the real estate business. Having just read Hill's book, I knew I needed to study under an expert in my chosen field if I wanted to be successful. Since I had no money for college (and didn't want to go, anyway), in my mind I saw Ron's offer as a golden opportunity to get an education for free.

I accepted his offer on the spot. I did not stay long at his house and quickly went home to tell my parents the news. The conversation with my dad went something like this:

"Dad, I got a new job today."

"Great, what does it pay?"

"Um, nothing, but I will learn a lot."

"Are you out of your mind, accepting a job without pay?"

I explained that I wanted to try it. Then I really pissed him off when I said, "Oh, and I am not going to go to community college this year because if I am working all day for free with Ron, and nights and weekends at the fitness center, I will have no time for college."

I did not have the money to pay for college anyway, so it made sense for me to skip it at that time. My parents, however, didn't see it that way. Unsurprisingly, their reaction was: "Get out!"

Talk about crazy. Within a few weeks, I moved out of my parents' house and into an apartment with my girlfriend. I was 18, with no money, no higher education, and a non-paying job. This was a brilliant start!

On August 21, 1983, I got into my 1968 Volkswagen (with no air-conditioning) and drove to my first day of work at Ron's company. It was a very hot day, and I remember thinking to myself, "Oh crap! I do not own a suit; what if I need a suit? I have no money for that. What will I do if my new non-paying job requires one?" (Mercifully, no suit was needed.)

I survived my initial days learning about real estate, and I really enjoyed myself. Over the next few months, I learned how the real estate business worked and how loans were made to purchase properties, and I began to understand what contributions I could make.

During the day, I learned and worked for free, and at night and on the weekends, I worked at the Merritt Athletic Club for minimum wage. So here I was, now 19 years old, learning the real estate and mortgage business, working for free by day and for very little on nights and weekends. I would go home from a long day to the apartment that I shared with my girlfriend and sit on the lawn chairs that doubled as our living room furniture.

Yet somehow, I knew that this was the right path for me.

The Turning Point

About four months into my new job, Ron agreed to pay me $150 per week. I cleared $115.14 after taxes and thought I was really moving up on the economic scale. One day, Ron asked me to come with him to see a seminar by Zig Ziglar. At the time, I had no idea who Zig Ziglar was, but I was really motivated by what I learned that day. So much so that I wanted to buy Mr. Ziglar's book, but I had no money.

I was a terrible reader, so I asked Ron if he would lend me the money to buy Mr. Ziglar's book on tape. That day I started listening to the tapes, and one of the principles I learned was that I needed to feed my mind with *only* useful information. This meant going back to reading self-help books.

What happened over the next three years was that I read about seventy books. I stopped listening to music on the radio and only listened to books on tape. I stopped watching TV, stopped reading the newspaper or watching the news, and I became completely submerged in educating myself in business, finance, sales, psychology, real estate, and really any subject I could get my hands on.

I started to interview as many successful people as I could locate by buying them breakfast, lunch, or dinner (cheap meals). The book *Think and Grow Rich*, along with a few years of study on wealth, real estate, finance, sales, and human behavior, acted as a catalyst and gave me an entirely new attitude towards life. I developed a radically different idea of what I needed to do each day and what actions I needed to take. I would talk to anyone and everyone I knew about what I was learning. I have a suspicion that I drove everyone crazy, and the truth is, I lost many friends over my obsession.

It was time to start putting all this information into practice and see if I could make it work for me. The Saturday after Thanksgiving in 1984, while Ron was visiting his dad in Florida, I asked Ron a question:

"Ron, would you agree to pay $150 for an ad in the money-to-loan section of the newspaper, if I agree to work all the leads that come in and split any commissions earned after the $150 is paid back?"

Ron agreed to pay for the ad. He put the expense on his credit card, and I placed the ad in the newspaper. What happened next demonstrates one of the reasons I truly love this country: In January 1985, I collected over $10,000 in mortgage broker fee revenue. This meant that after I repaid the $150 for the ad to Ron, I pocketed $5,000. I was nineteen years old, and I now had an entirely different perspective of the opportunities that were before me.

In one month, I went from earning $600 a month to $5,000. I thought I was rich.

In the full year of 1985, I earned $53,432, which was about the same salary as my dad earned with his college degree in computer science. From there, I worked around the clock, focusing on financial education and the mortgage and real estate business. I hired several of my friends from high school to come work for me and built up a successful mortgage operation within Ron's real estate company. My business continued to grow, and exactly four years to the day on August 21, 1987, I left Ron's company to begin my own.

At the age of 21, I became the youngest licensed mortgage broker in Maryland. That year I bought a four-bedroom, two-bath home with a pool, and several of my friends moved in with me and paid rent.

Here I was, living in my own four-bedroom home where the mortgage payment was paid for by my three friends, driving a luxury automobile, and making more money than my dad with his college degree.

Since those early days, I have had many successful years. I've bought over 250 real estate properties, directly or indirectly originated over six billion dollars in mortgage loans, and started and sold over a dozen companies, several for substantial profits.

Now, lest you think my entire journey was smooth sailing with constant profits, I want to confess that over the course of my career I made around a dozen bad business decisions that cost me millions—about $20 million to be precise. Let me be clear: My bad decisions have played as big a part in my formula for success as my good decisions have. In later chapters, I'll walk you through many of those bad decisions in detail, but here's a teaser of some of the catastrophes I've been through:

1. I had $6.1 million stolen from my company by two attorneys and a real estate developer.
2. I tried to acquire a bank; we spent $5 million and were denied, and the $5 million was not recoverable.

3. I sold a business for millions in all stock, and the company that bought me went out of business within 3 years. I ended up with pennies on the dollar.

I have learned a lot over the years as I have struck bad deals, hired bad employees, been responsible for bad business decisions, and made some plain old stupid mistakes. All of these cost me dearly at the time, but they also taught me how to be resilient. Most people that know me have heard me say that I paid millions of dollars for my education in business, real estate, and finance. I tell my story so that when I make my arguments regarding success, you can be confident that my experience was genuine and hard-earned. Because of everything I've been through, I can look back at all my successes and failures and tell you what I learned, how I got where I am today, what "to do," and what *not* "to do."

If He Can Do It...

Let me put this in perspective:

- I did not have a lot of money growing up.
- I went to public school.
- I did not attend college.
- I had a very low SAT score.

- I only received good grades in gym class and metal shop—neither of which were fields I ultimately went into.
- I have been diagnosed with Attention Deficit Disorder.
- I moved out of the house at age 18 and supported myself by working 2 jobs.
- I received no financial support or subsidy from my parents after the age of 16.

However...

- I read *Think and Grow Rich*—**that caused an action.**
- I chose to work without pay in the real estate business—**that caused an action.**
- While I was working without pay during the day, I worked at nights and weekends to support myself—**that caused an action.**
- I decided to spend 3 years reading, educating, learning, and growing in specific areas—**that caused an action.**
- I suggested placing an ad in the local newspaper to drive in opportunities for split profits—**that caused an action.**

- I decided to become my own boss at age 21—**that caused an action.**
- I committed to learning from successful people—**that caused an action.**
- I took many risks and was willing to fail—**that caused an action.**
- I made tons of mistakes along the way—**that caused an action.**

You might argue I had help from others or that I was lucky. You'd be right; there are times when I did strike gold or had amazing people reach into my life. The same will be true for you. Some days you're going to be at the right place at the right time, and other days you'll feel like you got the short end of the stick. We can neither control nor prevent that, but we can be prepared for it.

This book will show you that there is actually a formula behind the "luck"—that what you do with your luck (or lack thereof) is what will shape your success. As we go through my journey—and the journeys of other successful people—I will show you not only *what* happened, but also *how* and *why* it happened.

Let me be clear: Your financial journey will not be the same as mine. You may not have the same opportunities I did. But you don't need to have the same opportunities to have the same success. That's because my specific *circumstances* and *opportunities* are not only what made my success; it was the specific *attitude* and *actions* that I responded with that greatly created my success as well. Those attitudes and actions are something that anyone can learn and apply to their lives, regardless of the individual opportunities they are presented with.

An Attitude of Wealth

In fact, I believe that attitude is far more valuable than any amount of wealth you might acquire in life.

People are often surprised to hear me say this, since I deal in six- and seven-figure numbers every day, but I firmly believe that the person you become is more important than the items you own. Money is important, and it does us no good to deny that fact. But at the end of the day, money is still just a tool.

What you do with that tool will vary. Maybe you have specific goals you want to achieve—a house you want to buy, a car you want to drive. Most people want security, both for themselves and their children. Other people want the freedom to focus on doing what they love in life.

Many of these goals are critical for the healthy development of ourselves and our children. For example, I think a stable financial system is essential for your family, because a stable financial system allows you to provide the proper environment for your family's growth: proper healthcare, proper nurturing, proper education (including financial intelligence), a proper value system (leading by example as a hard worker), and many more attributes that are the by-products of a wealth-focused life.

That is why I encourage everyone to rethink their attitude about wealth. Wealth *is* accessible to you, and you owe it to yourself and your family to pursue it. That is also why, throughout this book, we will set goals and strive to reach a specific level of net worth.

But the thing to remember is that, while you are achieving these goals, you are also *becoming*. You are becoming a person who manages money, rather than someone whose money controls them. You are becoming a person who is focused, diligent, and passionate. You are becoming financially intelligent. You are becoming skilled. You are also growing a value for yourself and a value for healthy mindsets and habits. You are developing an attitude of abundance. Once you develop that attitude, you can be happy, healthy, and wealthy in *all* areas of your life, regardless of the circumstances and opportunities life throws at you.

So let's get started.

Creating wealth requires you to mix the right amount of effort, mindset, and formula.

THREE

The Wealth Creation Formula

When we really get down to brass tacks, the process for building wealth is quite rudimentary. There's no witchcraft or voodoo involved. You don't need to inherit hundreds of thousands of dollars; you don't have to work in big tech; and you don't have to strike it lucky with stocks. There's no complicated terminology; all the math can be done with a basic calculator; and you definitely don't need four years of college to understand it. It's my goal that, by the end of this book, you have a firm grasp on all the basic principles you need to know about wealth creation, as well as a clear, actionable plan for how to activate them in your own life.

First, let's establish a handful of important terms:

- **Income** refers to money coming in monthly, whether that be from salaries, freelance work, interest, profits from a business, etc.
- **Investable income** refers to the amount of income dedicated to being saved or invested. (We'll explain this in more detail in Chapters 5 and 6.)
- **Assets** are the tangible representations of wealth: bank accounts, real estate, stocks, businesses, and other valuables like gold, art, and expensive jewelry. In other words, an asset is either money or something that represents a monetary value. (We'll talk about managing these in Chapter 7.)
- **Leverage** refers both to maximizing resources to make a profit and to using debt to obtain assets. (We'll dive into this in Chapter 8.)
- **Net worth** is calculated by subtracting the total value of your liabilities (debts) from the total value of your assets (bank accounts, real estate, etc.). In other words: **Assets - Liabilities = Net Worth**

The most important term we need to define, however, is **wealth**. We discussed this in Chapter 1, but it bears repeating because I can't tell you the number of people I meet who have not taken the time to define wealth for themselves. Many of them keep earning more only to find themselves just spinning the hamster wheel faster and faster.

Defining wealth can be difficult because people have different impressions about what being wealthy means. Furthermore, we often correlate wealth with a certain *lifestyle*, when in reality lifestyle has nothing to do with whether or not someone is factually wealthy. For example, we all associate a Lamborghini with wealth, but not everyone who is wealthy drives a Lamborghini. It's also possible to own a Lamborghini and be in a tremendous amount of debt over it, which definitely isn't wealth!

That's why I define **wealth** as: *"a predictable, sustainable income amount consistent with your specific desires that is obtained both actively and passively through an accumulation of net worth."*

In other words, my definition of wealth is similar to many people's idea of **financial freedom**. Whether income is considered "active" or "passive" depends on how much time you are directly exchanging to earn that income. We'll discuss this more in Chapters 8 and 9.

You'll notice two things about my definition of wealth. The first is that it is quantified by *your* desired lifestyle. This is why wealth means different things to different people, and why wealth is not limited to certain professions. I say this because I don't want you to discount yourself from pursuing wealth either because you're in a low-earning profession or because you have "simple tastes." You don't need to work in finance or big tech to be wealthy. You don't have to live like the stereotypical "ultra rich" you see on TV to be wealthy. And you do *not* get to excuse yourself from being wealthy just because you have no desire to drive a fancy car or buy a bigger house. Wealth accomplishes so much more than buying status symbols. It affords you security and freedom from financial worry; it buys you back the time to spend on things you value; and it affords you deeply rewarding experiences, like providing financial peace for your children and grandchildren.

The second thing you'll notice about my definition is that it emphasizes net worth. That is because, as we've discussed, your level of income has little to do with whether or not you have sustainable wealth. Net worth is the only reliable, quantifiable indicator of wealth, and that's the rubric we'll be using to set our goals and measure our progress.

In the next chapter, we'll discuss how *much* net worth is truly wealthy and set an obtainable, actionable net worth goal for ourselves. For now, understand that when we say we are going to build wealth, we are talking about increasing our overall net worth.

With those basic definitions out of the way, we can now lay down the entire formula for wealth creation in a single sentence:

The Wealth Creation Formula

Income *x* Assets *x* Leverage *x* Time = Wealth Creation

It really is that simple! Those four variables—income, assets, leverage, and time—make up the formula for wealth creation. Although we're going to spend a great deal of time dissecting each variable and exploring how to enable them in our lives, the process for developing wealth *always* boils down to some combination of those four components. And when I say always, I mean always. Every act of wealth accumulation, from a child saving pennies in a piggy bank to Kylie Jenner selling millions of dollars' worth of lipstick, uses some iteration of that exact formula.

That is, in fact, why I talk about wealth creation in the language of a "formula" of "variables." Like any formula of variables (such as X = A+B+C+D), you can use different combinations of variables to get the same result. By the same token, you can also pick any number to be the value of "X" (net worth in our case); once you know your desired solution, you can calculate what variables you need to get there. "X" could equal 8, but it could also equal 20, 500, or even 1,000,000.

This is why I can be so confident that the wealth formula can apply to anyone in any situation, and why it's so ludicrous to limit wealth creation to certain professions or income levels. Although there are always more efficient ways to do things, and I will always make recommendations based on what will build the most wealth in the shortest time with the least effort, there are also no "wrong answers." You can endlessly customize each variable to meet your needs, goals, and resources, and the rest of this book will be spent showing you how to do just that.

Let's start by getting a basic definition for each variable and giving each an abbreviation so we can easily refer to them throughout the book.

The Four Variables

Investable Income (vA)

Variable "A" (vA) is **income**. Income can be generated from a variety of sources. The most common is, of course, the paycheck from our salaried jobs, freelance work, and side gigs. But income can also be generated through earning interest, collecting profits or royalties from a company we own or have a stake in, or selling an asset like stock, real estate, or business.

The purpose of solving the income variable is to have money to acquire assets, which we'll discuss next. This is why we'll primarily talk about **investable income** throughout the book, or the amount of money dedicated to saving or investing. If you earn $20 and then go buy groceries with it, you haven't added to your net worth. That's why we can't confuse our gross salary with our investable income, and why we'll spend the next chapter assessing how our money is being used.

Many people spend most or all of what they earn each month, which means they never solve their vA or increase their overall net worth. Ultimately, this has less to do with how *much* you make and everything to do with how you use the money that comes in. As the age-old wisdom says, "It's not about how much you make. It's about how much you save." Let me be very clear, however: Saving cash alone probably won't produce the net worth you need to be financially free. That's where the next variable comes in.

Acquisition of Assets (vB)

Variable "B" (vB) is **assets**. The word "assets" is one that many people trip over, partially because they don't have any, and partially because they don't know what they are. An asset is merely money or something that represents a monetary value. An asset can be something as simple as cash or a savings account—a piggy bank full of pennies is technically an asset!

When a child sells lemonade and saves up the quarters to buy a video game, they are using income (vA, selling lemonade) to acquire assets (vB, the jar of quarters) to reach their desired solution (wealth, a video game).

Our hypothetical lemonade story clearly demonstrates that the wealth creation formula isn't complex. If you wanted to simply work and generate a certain amount of surplus income each month (vA) which you put in a savings account until you retired (vB), you could, in theory, become a millionaire. In fact, many people have done that, using the benefits of compounding over time; they've started saving early, either in cash or through a simple retirement plan, and allowed the money to accumulate.

However, there are far more efficient (and profitable) ways of accumulating wealth than just stuffing cash in a mattress. There are dozens of asset strategies that can generate wealth: stocks, real estate, lending, and business ownership, just to name a few. Each of these has its merits and requires different amounts of active involvement and monetary investment. Finding the asset strategy that works for you involves assessing your competencies, interests, and desires, which is why we spend a great deal of time in Chapter 7 exploring some of the asset options and helping you discover the one that's right for you and your family.

Use of Leverage (vC)

Variable "C" (vC) is **leverage**. Solving this variable is all about maximizing your assets and resources, or making them work for you more effectively. Leverage can come in many shapes and sizes (people, money, time, and energy, just to name a few), but the primary goal of leverage is to help you acquire more asset value (vB) with less investable income (vA).

As we discussed, you could, technically, just stuff money in a mattress until you reached your first million. But not only would that be extraordinarily unsafe, it would also severely limit your ability to multiply your wealth. If your wealth creation strategy is dependent solely on how much money you can squirrel away each month, then your growth will always be limited by how much cash you can squeeze out of your budget.

This is why many people fail to build significant amounts of wealth, even if they have savings or retirement plans. They do not learn how to make their money earn more money, and they trick themselves into believing wealth "isn't for them" because they do not have enough surplus income. This is why we'll spend time in Chapter 8 discussing how leverage and other basic financial principles work, and how you can use them to generate exponential growth, regardless of your income level.

Short & Long-Term Use of Time (vD)

Variable "D" (vD) is **time**. Time is tricky because it continually slips by us without notice, but the effective use of time will make or break your wealth-building strategy.

There are two sides to using time wisely. First and foremost, time defines the rate by which all of the other variables perform. If we work for a salary (vA) and save $1,000 a month (vB), the length of time we stick to this savings plan determines our result. Interest compounds over time; the value of a business is built over time; mortgages are paid down over time. All of these values are contingent upon time.

But time is also a resource in and of itself. When we talk about time, it's important not to think of it as a static resource that just flows past in the background. Every day we are given 24 hours, and we must spend, waste, or invest that time intentionally. Yes, the hands of the clock will keep ticking whether we do anything or not, but it is up to us to control our time and use it to our advantage. The importance of time cannot be overstated.

Endless Solutions

Now you understand why it is helpful to discuss wealth creation in terms of a "mathematical" formula of variables. Just in the last few pages we have mentioned several unique combinations of variables that could be used to generate wealth. A child saving pennies is using the income variable, the asset variable, and the time variable. The average corporate retirement plan uses all four variables, with a heavy emphasis on compounding interest over time. Someone who receives a large inheritance might just be using the income variable, while someone who builds and sells a business for profit might be primarily using the asset variable.

Generally speaking, we're going to use income and leverage to acquire assets, which then use leverage and time to generate more income and assets. This is the simplest application of the wealth formula, and the one we'll primarily focus on throughout the book. There are always outliers, but most effective strategies are going to use all four variables in a similar fashion.

However, before we can dive in and start designing a path to wealth, there are two more factors we need to consider. First, we need to determine the "solution" to our equation, or the amount of net worth we want to generate. We also need to have a thorough understanding of our current financial situation, or the "range" of numbers with which we are currently working. Then, and only then, can you build a personalized plan to determine how to get from where you are today to your place of financial freedom.

Answering these questions involves more than just picking an arbitrary number and adding up the contents of all your bank accounts. It requires a thorough assessment of your financial state, which is exactly what we'll do in the next chapter.

CASE STUDY #1

John S., Maryland

About the Case Studies

A true rag-to-riches story always motivates and excites me. When real people go against the odds and bend the universe to give them what they want, it reminds me that anything is possible and encourages me to strive for my next goal. If you also find such stories to be inspirational, you are in for a treat, because throughout this book you will hear the unique stories of seven self-made millionaires.

These will be real individuals who have achieved a net worth of more than two million dollars. As we've been discussing, no two paths to wealth are completely identical, and that fact is on full display in each case study. Each person took a different journey to wealth that was unique based on their skills and opportunities. Some achieved their first million early; some developed it slowly. Some grew businesses and others sold stock. Some had a college education; others didn't. All of them used the wealth creation formula in a creative and profitable way.

As you read each story, I encourage you to notice how each person utilized the variables of the wealth creation formula. Take notes. What about each story inspires you? Could you see yourself using similar strategies? These people shared their lives with me so that you could borrow from their successes and write your own rags-to-riches triumph. So dig in and remember that this *can* and *will* be you one day.

Case Study #1: John S., Maryland

When I first interviewed John, he was 69 years old. He was a high school graduate with no college education whatsoever. His grades in high school were straight Bs—points for consistency, I suppose. If you're wondering why I would choose to interview John, it's because his net worth at the time was **five million dollars,** none of which was inherited from family.

Crazy right? I was interested as well. John is currently retired, but he used to be a mechanic and owned his own shop.

When I asked him about his average annual income over the past three years, he responded: "It's $160k." But what really got me excited was the realization that *all* of that income was from passive sources.

John started out by working several odd jobs. His first job was delivering newspapers. His second was washing cars, and at age 17 he was hired to work in a gas station. Finally, when he was 20 years old, he started working for someone else as a mechanic. He worked for 6 years and gathered all the knowledge he needed to open his own garage. So when the owner of his garage prepared to sell the building, John was able to seize his opportunity. At the age of 26, he became the owner-operator of his own shop.

That one move allowed him to produce a solid cash flow, a strong vA strategy. Some of those assets he poured back into the shop, ultimately buying the building he leased—a vB solution. The rest was invested into passive income streams. As the owner-operator, John ran the shop for 39 years and retired at the age of 65.

What makes John's story truly inspirational is how little he started with when it comes to investable income. Although buying the shop was an excellent investment, operating costs left him with shockingly little investable income for the first few years. But as his business grew, John dedicated himself to exponentially growing his investable income. His journey went like this:

John's Age	Annual investable Income
20-30	$0-$5k
30-40	$10k-$12k
40-50	$15k-$20k
50-60	$25k+

Even though he started small, John knew that it was crucial to begin early, so he purchased public stocks and bonds with as much investable income as he could afford. Ultimately, much of John's net worth was created by his mechanics shop, but he continued to invest in passive income streams, including rental properties and commercial buildings. It was those investments that continued to grow and allowed him to retire on a $160,000 annual salary of entirely passive income.

I asked John what advice he'd give the younger generation on the path of wealth. He replied, "I have three pieces of advice to share, all three of which I followed in my own life: First, I always saved money and invested it. Second, I never paid credit card interest. Third, I always doubled up on house payments.

"In addition, there were two primary decisions that defined my journey to wealth. First, I built a successful mechanic shop business. Second, I bought the building my shop was in, as well as additional rental properties."

In summary, John utilized his mechanic skills and took the risk of becoming a self-employed business owner to generate a variable vA solution. He then solved variable vB by buying the commercial building, other rental properties, and stocks.

If you invest money without intention, you'll just go the wrong way faster.

FOUR

Assessing Your Financial Self

To successfully complete any journey, we need to know not only where we are but also where we're going. The beauty of the wealth creation formula is that it can apply to anyone, regardless of their current financial situation. But if we don't know what our current financial situation is—let alone have a clear grasp of where we want to end up—we'll end up grinding our gears and wasting money.

The goal of this chapter is to help you set a concrete goal for wealth building and take a thorough, honest stock of your financial health. This will require doing some "homework" and digging into your accounts; you're going to have to look up your insurance and mortgage policies, tally debt, and calculate the value of any assets you own. It will take some time, and depending on how much you enjoy crunching numbers, it may not be fun.

But I strongly encourage you not to skip this chapter, no matter where you think you stand financially. Even if you know you're running a budget deficit each month and have significant debts to wrangle, still take the time to detail all of your expenses and liabilities. You may find that you have more assets to work with than you realize, and even if you don't, the more you know about where your money is going, the more you can control its flow.

On the other hand, maybe you're doing well financially and have already acquired some assets. For all I know, you could be reading this book and already have several hundred thousand—or more!—in stocks, real estate, and pure cash. I still encourage you to fill out all of the assessments thoroughly. Doing so will allow you to see how your assets are divided and ascertain what vehicles are generating you the most (and least) amount of income. Once you know where your strengths truly lie, you will be in a position to multiply that wealth exponentially. Throwing money sporadically at investment opportunities never yields the most efficient results, whether you're dealing in three figures or six, so take the time to organize your money and understand what you're working with.

Where We're Going

Before we dig into the nitty-gritty of your current financial situation, let's decide where we're going. Like any formula of variables, the wealth creation formula has an infinite number of "solutions"—you can use the same principles to generate $100,000 worth of wealth or twenty million. To put the formula to work for us, we need to define our desired "solution." We need to set a concrete goal to aim for. Simply put, we have to put a dollar amount on success.

The trouble with words like "success" and "wealth" is that they mean different things to different people at different times in their lives. If I asked *"What does wealth look like to you?"*, you'd give me an answer unique to your goals and situation. Now imagine I asked 18-year-old you the same question; I bet I'd get a much different answer. The same goes for my "younger" readers; how do you think you might answer that question when you're 30, 45, or 60?

This is why I think it's important to put a fixed dollar amount on success, rather than focusing on other material goals like buying a particular house, paying for your kid's college education, or even retiring on a certain amount. All of those goals are good, and they factor into our picture of wealth, but they are transient. What happens once we fulfill those temporary goals? What happens if situations change and our goals are rendered irrelevant (say, for instance, your kid is like me and chooses not to go to college)? How do we define wealth then? If we allow our definition of success to be dictated by temporal material goals, we may find ourselves stranded if situations change. Worse, we may find that we crippled our long-term success by throwing all of our resources at a short-term need.

So if we aren't limiting our long-term goal by the cost of a college education or our dream house, what should our magic number be? Although you're free to choose your own path in life, with my experience I strongly recommend making it your goal **to have a net worth of one million dollars ($1,000,000).**

If you balked at that number, that's okay. Many people can't imagine ever being worth one million dollars, or even half that. But I *implore* you not to limit yourself right now. As soon as you discount yourself, as soon as you tell yourself that it's "not for you," you sabotage your chances of success. If you tell yourself that you'll never have a net worth of one million, you've decided your own fate. You've taken the ski lift down the mountain instead of choosing to climb it. You've sacrificed your opportunity to become wealthy before you even got started.

Nothing in life is guaranteed, I get that. I can't promise you that you'll one day be worth one million. But I *can* promise you that if you decide you can't do it, you won't.

We'll discuss attitude and self-talk further in the coming chapters, but now—in this moment right here—is where you begin to shape your financial self-image. What you tell yourself in this moment, as you're putting your first goal down on paper, will define your future. So take this courageous first step with me. Find a piece of paper—any paper—but make sure it's a real, physical piece of paper. In the biggest, boldest letters you can draw, write: "My goal is to be worth $1,000,000." Now write that twice more on two other sheets of paper, and post them in three different places that are meaningful to you. It could be in your journal, on a sticky note on your mirror, or on a poster pasted on the wall in your bedroom. If your goal lives only in a digital space like your phone or computer, it won't feel as real. Put it somewhere in your physical space where you'll see it every day.

There. Your journey to financial success has officially begun. And you've accomplished something many people fail to do: set a concrete, measurable, attainable goal.

This goal is going to change over time, and that's *good*. At a bare minimum, as you acquire more wealth, I hope you are inspired to gain more! When you reach the day that you're worth one million dollars, I hope you're inspired to go for five million.

You might be wondering, if goals are so transient, why set them at all? That brings us back to the conversation we had at the beginning of this chapter: We have to know where we're going before we start a journey. We can't "solve" our equation of variables if we don't have our projected solution. A lot of research has been done on the psychological impact of having a concrete goal; it is incredibly difficult to succeed without it. So don't skip this crucial step. Set your goal, put it in multiple places, and commit to it, mentally and emotionally.

This brings us to our next order of business: putting a timeframe on our goal. Having a concrete number is good, but without a "deadline," we still run the risk of spinning our wheels and missing our goal. If we have a timeframe, we'll be better able to break our plan into achievable action steps and measure our progress along the way.

So what timeframe should we put on becoming wealthy? My recommendation is to **plan on achieving one million dollars of net worth within twenty years**. If you're older, you may consider aiming for a shorter time span, and there are many ways you can accelerate your progress.

On the other hand, if you're younger, you may be tempted to believe that you have more time. And while you might have an extra twenty years before you want to retire, why would you postpone achieving your goal by another two decades? If you can achieve one million dollars in net worth by your 40s, think of how much *more* you can do before you retire. Don't take the lazy route (because that's what it is) and give yourself more time; aim for twenty years, and then use the extra time to multiply.

Now you may be asking, why twenty years? I suggest twenty years because it allows sufficient time for assets to appreciate and enables you to fully develop your long-term wealth-building strategy. We'll discuss this more later, but a central component of effective wealth building is developing a long-term asset strategy. This is not a get-rich-quick scheme, nor is it a fix-it-and-forget-it retirement plan. This is about developing an effective, profitable asset strategy that will cause your money to work for you and continue to build wealth long into your future. These asset vehicles take time to develop and mature, which is why twenty years is a good target for most people.

So there you have it: your concrete, achievable, measurable goal for wealth building. You have decided that you are going to have one million dollars in net worth within twenty years. Congratulations! Write that goal down (yes, again), and let's get started on the first step of achieving that goal.

Documenting Where You Are

Now that we know where we're going, it's time to determine where we are. I'm going to walk you through the process of calculating your current financial state and ascertaining what stage of the wealth-building journey you are in. We're also going to delve into your core competencies, personality, and interests, so that we can begin to personalize your path to wealth.

But before we begin, I want to remind you that all of this is for your benefit. The purpose of these exercises is to help you gain control of your money and develop an effective, personalized action plan for achieving wealth. The more accurate and detailed your responses are, the more empowered you are to be successful. There should be no shame in this process. No one is going to grade you on this "homework." I'm not going to see these numbers; your friends, your parents, and your in-laws don't have to, either. This is just between you and your money. Omitting expenses, fudging numbers, or guessing on the balances of your debts will only hurt *you*. You're not protecting yourself (or anyone else) by being dishonest or lackadaisical with this process. So stop judging yourself (because that's really the issue, if we're honest), kick the kids and the dog out of the room so you can focus, and take the time to be thorough and precise with your responses.

To complete these assessments, we're going to use two online tools that you can find at the following website:

Wealthtools.WorrytoWealthBook.com

Each tool has a video tutorial to help you use it effectively. Take the time to watch them before continuing.

The first tool is called the **Money Positioning System (MPS)**; this is Money Club's primary budgeting and financial assessment tool. At the site above, you can download an interactive version of the tool and enter in your own numbers. The MPS is an all-in-one financial management tool that will help you in two major ways:

1. It will determine and track your net worth, and
2. It will determine and track your monthly budget.

The second tool is an income self-assessment called **Your Way to $20k** that is designed to help you discover potential avenues to increase your investable income to $20,000 a year. Why $20,000 a year? Because that's generally the rate you'll need to save and invest over time to achieve a million dollar net worth in 10-20 years. We'll break that number down further in Chapter 6.

As you answer questions about your strengths and interests, this tool will not only help you discover your most *effective* means of producing money, but also the ones you'll most *enjoy*. We'll use this tool more in Chapter 6, but I encourage you to go ahead and take a stab at it now so you can start thinking about your strengths and interests with regards to money. You can always go back and take the assessment again later.

Tracking Your Net Worth

Let's begin by using the Money Positioning System to determine your current net worth. To do so, you'll add up the value of all your assets and subtract your total amount of liabilities. The number you get is your current net worth. Remember, our goal is to get to one million dollars in net worth, so your results from this worksheet will immediately show you how far you are from that goal. Keep that number handy; we'll come back to it at the end of the chapter.

If you find you have a very low—or even negative—net worth, don't get frustrated. You are definitely not alone. But you will not be here for long; if you apply yourself to the principles in this book, within twenty years (maybe less!) you will be in the top 20% for net worth nationwide[4].

---

[4] Based on 2019 numbers: https://www.federalreserve.gov/publications/files/scf20.pdf

As you do this exercise, you'll find there are several fields asking you to detail the specifics of your assets and liabilities. This is where you will want to take your time and be precise. Make the effort to check on your current credit card balances, look up interest rates, and estimate the current market value of your home. All of this information will be critical in developing an effective financial plan during the early stages of your journey, so the more research you do here, the more time you'll save later.

In addition to giving you control over your liabilities, the MPS also shows you which of your assets are the most valuable and profitable. As you get into the later stages of your financial journey and begin to maximize assets, you may find that you want to build on an asset you already possess. So keep these numbers handy; they are your complete diagnostic of your money, and you'll reference them often.

Tracking Your Monthly Budget

As you fill out the MPS, you'll also be completing a budget. In the most basic sense, a budget tells you where your money is going each month, and much of our journey will be spent adjusting this flow so that our money is multiplied rather than wasted. But even more importantly, a budget tells you if you have any excess income after expenses. As of today, that extra money is now your **investable income**.

We'll talk extensively about this in Chapter 6, but a core part of our strategy will be generating investable income, which will be fed into an asset strategy so it can earn more money. That's why it's critical that we have an effective budget so that we know exactly how much money we have to invest each month.

For a budget to be effective, however, it has to be both realistic and thorough. People fail with budgeting for two main reasons: They set goals that are not realistic, or they do not account for all of their regular spending. It does you no good to set a $200 monthly food budget for a family of 5 when you know that you will spend more, and failing to budget for incidental items like veterinary care for your pet or a once-every-six-months hair appointment can derail even the most diligent spender. Because of this, using the MPS will not be a one-time exercise. You will need to continually go back and adjust the numbers as your situation changes, so don't be afraid to go back and edit your budget if you find unaccounted-for expenses. I personally recommend that you review your budget once a month; the more diligent you are with your budget, the more proactive you will be with your money.

For now, though, don't get too caught up in trying to perfect your budget. Focus on charting your **actual** expenses by estimating, to the best of your ability, what you spent on each category last month. If something is an annual expense—like homeowner's insurance—divide it by 12 to get a monthly payment amount. The goal, at this stage, is to figure out how much investable income you **currently** have based on your current expenses and income, so focus on getting that raw number. We'll dig into our budget in more detail in Chapter 5.

If you've already been using a budget—and I commend you for doing so—or have a different budgeting chart or app that you prefer to use, go ahead. It does not matter so much *how* you budget as long as you *do* budget. As long as you can get a concrete number for your investable income—the total remaining after you subtract your monthly income from expenses—it doesn't matter which budgeting method you use.

If you find you have little excess income—or perhaps you're even running a deficit each month—don't panic. Again, you're not alone. Chapters 5 and 6 will be spent fixing this problem and getting you to the place where you have the right amount of investable income for your stage of the journey. Whatever your final number is, highlight it and keep it handy; we'll come back to it at the end of this chapter.

Your Way to $20k: An Income Self-Assessment

This next exercise requires a bit more self-reflection. These aren't financial questions so much as they are personality questions. This is where we start digging into who you are as a person—financially, professionally, and mentally-emotionally. You're going to ask yourself questions about your career, your dreams, and the ability of both to make you money. Be honest with yourself; there are no consequences to any of your answers at this stage. Relax, take your time, and remember that each step is a step towards your financial improvement.

You may not have concrete answers to some of these questions. That's okay. We're going to come back to this line of thinking in Chapter 6 when we discover the income strategy that's best for you. Our ultimate goal is to determine the personalized path that will effectively build wealth for *you*. This means finding an income strategy that you're not only *capable* of doing well, but that you also *enjoy* doing.

You may already have a clear idea of what your long-term strategy will be. Maybe you're a business owner, and you know you can expand into a franchise. Maybe you've dabbled in real estate and enjoyed the process. If so, you have a head start. Now is the time to start digging into the reality of your vision and asking yourself questions like: Do I need more education? Will I need business capital and/or partners to expand my ventures? Is my day job competing with my long-term strategy for time and resources? Fill out the questions to the best of your ability and start making a list of topics you need to research and further questions you need to answer.

On the other hand, maybe you have absolutely no idea what will work for you. You might be in a career you hate. Maybe you have a talent or dream but have no idea how to make it profitable. That's okay—again, there's no "wrong" answers at this stage. The key is that you start asking the questions *now*, instead of in 20-40 years when you've spent your life on a career that wasn't fulfilling. Have those honest conversations with yourself. Talk with friends, family, or a counselor. Take additional personality or career assessment tests. Start exploring all the options that are available to you. In Chapter 7 we'll discuss several different asset strategies and help you find the one that's perfect for you.

Although this assessment tool is important for everyone, I want to especially encourage my "younger" readers. If you're in your teens or twenties, I want to congratulate you for thinking proactively about your future. You have the irreplaceable opportunity to pick a profitable, enjoyable career path before you get started. If you haven't gone to college yet, that's even more power to you! Really take the time to explore yourself with this tool, and involve trusted parents and mentors. The stronger your foundation when you begin, the faster you'll find your way to $20k and beyond.

The Wealth Creation Stages

Now that we're armed with a thorough assessment of our financial state, we're ready to begin our journey towards wealth. As we've mentioned, no two paths to financial success are exactly alike, but everyone's journey to wealth goes through the same five basic stages based on net worth:

- **Stage 1: Worry** ($0 - $50k net worth)
- **Stage 2: Foundation** ($50k - $250k net worth)
- **Stage 3: Stability** ($250k - $1M net worth)
- **Stage 4: Growth** ($1M-$3M net worth)
- **Stage 5: Freedom** (over $5M net worth)

Although each stage has the overall goal of building net worth, the focus of each stage changes. Someone who is in the Worry stage should be using their time, money, and other resources in a very different way from someone who is in the Stability or Freedom stage.

The chart below provides guidelines for the target goals of each stage. There are targets for investable income, passive income, and the recommended amount of time spent learning and earning each day of the work week. Of course, real life doesn't always fit in a perfect box, so the lines between the stages are often blurred. For now, don't get hung up on specific numbers; we'll discuss each column in detail in the coming chapters.

Wealth Creation Stages

#	Stage	Total Net Worth Target	Monthly Investable Income Target	Monthly Passive Income Target	Time Spent Earning Each Day	Time Spent Learning Each Day
1	Leaving Worry Behind	>$0-$50k	$0-$500	N/A	10	2
2	Laying Your Foundation	$50k-$250k	$500-$1,600	$50	10	2
3	Creating Stability	$250k-$1M	$1,600-$3,000	$250	10	2
4	Building for Growth	$1M-$3M	$3,000-$8,000	$2,500	9	2
5	Unlocking Freedom	$3M+	$8,000+	$8,000	8	1

Now that we know where we are, we can begin the process of going from the Worry stage to the Growth stage and beyond. To make things easy to navigate, I've organized the material in this book into three progressive steps:

- **Step 1: Leave Worry Behind.** We'll use budget reduction and debt payoff to get ourselves on firm financial footing. (Chapter 5)

- **Step 2: Generate Investable Income.** We'll explore ways to increase our monthly income and free up resources for investment. (Chapter 6)
- **Step 3: Discover Your Asset Strategy.** We'll discover the long-term asset strategy that best fits our strengths and competencies so we can make our money work for us. (Chapter 7)

The "step" you should be focusing on depends on which "stage" of wealth creation you're in. To find out where to go next, use your net worth and monthly investable income—which you just calculated using the Money Positioning System—with the chart above to determine the appropriate stage.

Worry Stage. If you're in the Worry stage, again, you're in good company. Start on Step 1; we're going to dive right in and discover how to manage our income and expenses to get us on the right track.

Foundation Stage. Congratulations, you're off to a strong start. I encourage you to start in Step 1; even though you probably already have an effective budget, you might find that, with a little reduction, you can immediately free up enough monthly investable income to propel you into the next stage. Your primary focus, however, will probably be on Step

2, where we start looking at long-term strategies for developing investable income.

What if you have over $250,000 in net worth but less than $1,600 a month in investable income? Sometimes people find themselves—perhaps through inheritance or a profitable business venture—in a position where they have a decent amount of net worth but are still breaking even (or worse) on their monthly expenses. If this is the case, go to Step 1 and start at the beginning with budget reduction. If you are going to multiply the net worth that you already have, it's imperative that you free up that investable income each month. Furthermore, if you don't start increasing your monthly margin, you will eventually have to start using your net worth to maintain your lifestyle. Start at the beginning and be diligent; as soon as you start generating that monthly investable income, you'll be able to leverage your existing assets and hit the ground running.

If the reverse is true—you have $1,600 of investable income but a low net worth—I encourage you to work through the budget exercises in Step 1. First, you'll want to determine if there is a liability that is counteracting your income and preventing you from growing your overall net worth. Second, however, you'll want to have a strong grasp of your income streams so you can immediately start maximizing your most effective sources of revenue. This will help you as go through Step 2 and solidify your long-term plan for generating investable income. You want to make sure you're focusing your energies on a plan that serves your lifelong goals; working five jobs might get you $1,600 a month in investable income, but it is neither sustainable nor enjoyable. Once you have these tools under your belt, you'll be empowered to dive into Step 3 and pour that income into an asset strategy that will fulfill your long-term needs.

Stability Stage. If you're in the Stability stage, chances are you already have several asset strategies working for you. Now is the time to solidify and diversify to make sure you have a clear, well-defined path that will continue to build wealth for you over the next twenty years. Although I encourage you to still read Chapters 5 and 6, your main focus will be Step 3, where you will examine all your asset strategies and refine the ones that work best for you.

Growth and Freedom Stages. As mentioned earlier, my main focus with this book is on guiding people towards attaining their first one million in net worth. However, the same principles continue to operate no matter where you are on your journey; the same strategies that allow someone from the Foundation stage to graduate into the Stability stage can take you into the Growth stage and beyond. Your main focus will probably be Step 3; now is the time to reexamine your asset strategies and consider whether your money is being utilized to its full potential. However, we are never above learning something new. I encourage you to take the time and read the entire book; you never know when you'll discover a strategy that will liberate even more of your money.

Now that you know where you're at and where you're going, let's dive right in. It's time to build wealth!

CASE STUDY #2

Henry S., Pittsburgh, PA

When I interviewed Henry, he was 59 years old. He was working as the general manager of a print company and had a net worth of 2.1 million dollars. None of his wealth was inherited. When I asked him about his average annual income over the past three years, he responded, "It's been between $350k and $400k, with $150k from passive income."

Despite having a bachelor's degree in marketing and finance, he freely admits his grades weren't phenomenal. In both high school and college he typically earned Bs and Cs.

Like John, Henry worked different positions over the course of his journey. His first job was as a manager at the London Fog Coat Company. The second was as a general manager at Solo Cup Company. His third job was as a manager at a printing company; he was promoted from within to his current position of general manager. Unlike John, however, Henry said that he never thought of himself as someone who would run his own business, so he never pursued any self-employment options.

Growing up, Henry made a dedicated effort to surround himself with positive financial influencers. He never received any helpful influence from his family because they were ignorant of the financial world. Instead, he intentionally searched for that influence somewhere else. He found it from four key people: two financially smart friends he made in college, one supportive teacher, and one former boss who was a formidable risk-taker. Nevertheless, Henry had to mainly teach himself through discipline and personal responsibility.

After getting his degree, Henry worked rigorously hard to achieve as many high-income jobs as possible to build his variable vA solution. Until his late 20s all of his income went into a 401k. Here is a table below that illustrates how his income grew over time:

Henry's Age	Annual Investable Income
20-30	$0-10k
30-40	$15k-$30k (maxed by his 401k)
40-50	$15k-$30k
50-60	$120k-$170k

To create a variable vB solution, Henry invested that income in the following areas:

- He bought public stocks and bonds through his 401k; he did not buy any individual stocks.
- He bought his primary residence and had the mortgage paid off very quickly.
- Most recently, he has been investing in mortgages. In fact, this is how I came to meet him; Henry has been investing with me for the past twelve years.

Finally, I asked Henry for any advice about wealth creation that he wanted to share. He gave me the following generous list:

- Work very hard.
- Get educated on investing, taxes, and budgeting, and talk to anyone that is self-made. "How you end up is a summation of the choices you have made," he says, so talk to people who are successful and ask them what choices they made.
- Don't be a victim, and be prepared for your moments of opportunity.
- Avoid going into debt unless it is for an investment; do not borrow unless it is for an appreciable asset.

- Start investing early.

Additionally, Henry boiled down his path to wealth into three distinct components:

1. He listened to first-generation financially successful people and followed their advice.
2. He saved and invested as early as possible.
3. He stressed that living below his means was his greatest vehicle to success. As he was raising his income, he kept his expenses low so that his available investable income grew exponentially.

In summary, Henry utilized his education and hard work ethic to be a manager for many years. Meanwhile, he lived below his means with little debt to generate his variable vA solution. He then solved the variable vB investment strategy by buying as many public stocks as possible through his 401k, paying off his house, and investing in high-yielding mortgages.

What we do, say, and think about every minute of the day, week, month, or year produces what we get. If we do not like what we are getting, we should change what we are doing, saying, and thinking.

FIVE

Step 1: Leave Worry Behind

My guess is that most of you reading this book are worried about money, in some shape or form. It might be a long-term worry about something looming on the horizon: paying for your kids' college education, or having enough savings to retire. Maybe you're worried about the stability of your job or the future of the economy. Or maybe you're worried about something that's happening right now—like not being able to pay rent this month.

No matter what your current financial situation is, our goal with this chapter is to eliminate worry from our financial lives. We're going to accomplish this through budget reduction, eliminating high-interest debt, and building an emergency fund. But before you get hung up on bills and credit card balances, I want to remind you that eliminating the *emotion* of worry is actually the most important thing we'll do in this chapter. That's because we cannot make sound financial decisions when we're operating out of a place of fear.

We don't make good decisions when we are afraid. Someone who is financially fearful will often either "hoard" their resources and refuse to take the risks necessary to have successful investments, or they will spend erratically in an attempt to patch a problem or stave off the hurtful emotions. Fear can also cause people to focus on a symptom rather than a root cause; for example, they might run themselves ragged trying to pay down credit card debt without correcting the spending problem that caused the debt in the first place. Whatever the situation, we cannot grow our financial "selves" without first overcoming the crippling effects of fear and worry.

I can't promise you that you'll feel better instantly. You're going to need to make some immediate and significant changes to the way you handle money. You'll have to adjust the way you spend and save, and you will likely need to alter your lifestyle. You will need to be extremely diligent with yourself, especially for the first year. Much of this will not be fun in the moment, and it will require sustained discipline.

But I can promise you that, if you stick with it and get yourself on firm financial footing, you will begin to feel empowered with money. Step 1 is all about taking control of your financial life. Everything we accomplish in this chapter serves not only to free up resources—so that you can take care of your immediate needs *and* start investing for your future—but also to put you in the driver's seat. When we're in the Worry stage, all of that fear tries to dictate our financial decisions. By the time you graduate to Step 2, you'll be back in control of your money.

We have three main goals we want to accomplish in Step 1:

1. Pay off all high-interest (10% or greater) debt.
2. Build an emergency fund equal to 6 months of expenses.
3. Adjust our schedule to prioritize both earning and learning.

To do this, we're going to look at three key areas of our lives:

1. **Budget:** We're going to thoroughly examine our income and expenses so that we can not only live below our means but also accomplish our goals of paying off debt and building an emergency fund.

2. **Schedule:** We're going to evaluate how we're spending our time so we can shift our most valuable resource towards our most important goals.
3. **Education:** We're going to take a critical look at what we're feeding our minds and begin studying the behaviors and asset strategies that will make us money.

Let's get started.

Budgeting to Win

"Budget." It's an intimidating word that gives more people anxiety than the sound of nails on a chalkboard. Chances are, if you're in the Worry stage, you've either tried several budgets and failed, or your financial influencers have lectured you about having a budget without actually walking you through the process of creating and maintaining one. Either way, the mere mention of the word is enough to turn some people off.

But no matter what your experience was with budgeting in the past, our journey to financial freedom has to start here. I do not know a single person who became wealthy without first managing their daily expenses. You need to have a budget, and you need to have one that works for *you*.

I'm sure this isn't the first sermon you've heard about budgeting, nor will it be the last. I'm not trying to reinvent the wheel, nor do I pretend to be the definitive expert on budgeting. There are many excellent books and workshops on the art of budgeting, and if you find one that you like, use it! In fact, I encourage you to read as many books and listen to as many podcasts on budgeting and money management as you can. My goal in this chapter is not so much to tell you *how* to budget as it is to explain *why* you need to budget. Money Club has great online courses that teach personal finance in a very practical and relatable way, if you're looking for a good place to start.

First, let's demystify the word "budget." A budget is simply a cash flow plan. It details what money comes in, where that money goes, and evaluates if there's a surplus or deficit. Businesses have budgets. Organizations have budgets. Households and individuals have budgets.

When you create a budget for you or your family, your goal is to calculate how much money comes in—from paychecks, child support payments, and the like—and then decide what that money will be used for. A budget is *you* telling *your* money where it will go. Many people trip over budgeting because they forget that they are in control. A budget is not about denying yourself or simply throwing enough money at a beast (like credit card debt) to keep it quiet. That doesn't mean we won't choose to sacrifice some things we want in favor of things we need, but the key is that *we're* making the decision. We're setting the priorities.

That, in fact, is the best piece of advice I can give you in regards to budgeting: Set your priorities. When you look over your expenses, instead of asking yourself what you want or need, ask yourself what's most important to you. Once you have a clear sense of your priorities, you'll find it infinitely easier (and a lot less anxiety-inducing) to design a budget and stick with it.

Let me frame it this way. If you knew that, every time you upgraded to the latest iPhone, you condemned yourself to working at the soul-sucking job you hate for *another six months*, would you do it? Would the iPhone still be worth it to you if you knew that it would add time on your "indenture"? The answer is probably no, and once you recognize the correlation between your choices today and your future tomorrow, it becomes much easier to make wise decisions and feel confident in them.

The trouble is that it's difficult to see those long-term consequences when you're in the moment. It becomes even harder to sort out your priorities when you've got dozens of bills staring you in the face and you're trying to wrangle them into some semblance of a budget. That's why, before we revisit our budget, we need to take the time to hone our priorities.

We need to get them crystalized in our mind, so that when we open our budgeting app or checkbook, we can clearly see what's hindering our dreams.

So what should our priorities be? Obviously, "generating my first one million in net worth" is a good goal, but even that is a bit stoic. Ultimately, money is a tool, and simply gaining wealth for the sake of being rich is not a solid motivation. Instead, ask yourself *why* you want to be wealthy, or *what* you'd do with wealth and financial freedom once you had it. Here are some suggestions to get you thinking:

- I want to retire young so I can spend more time with my grandchildren.
- I want to leave a good inheritance to my children.
- I want to be able to focus on creating art.
- I want to buy my partner their dream home.
- I want my kids to go through college without debt.
- I don't want to ever struggle with paying rent again.
- I want to donate to charity.

There are no wrong answers to this question, and no motivation is too small or too big. Do you have a dream car you want to drive? Great! Do you want to adopt an orphan from overseas? Wonderful! What's important to you? What motivates you? What do you value in life? Get a piece of paper and write down everything you can think of. Then go through and circle the three that are *most* important to you.

Those three things, right there, are your priorities. Those three things define who you are as a person and why you do what you do. Consciously or otherwise, you make decisions based on those motivations. So get them in front of your face; make copies and hang them everywhere you'll see them on a daily basis. When the going gets tough and you have to make hard financial decisions, all the money advice in the world won't help you. It's your priorities that will dictate who you are and what you do.

Now, with your motivation list on the desk in front of you, go back to the budget section of the MPS that we completed in the previous chapter and look through each line item. Is your spending in each category supporting or distracting from your priorities? If it's distracting, what amount of spending in this category would better suit your goals?

Just this simple exercise can help many people find and patch the holes in their budget. But there are many other ways to get your budget under control, which we'll discuss in a moment.

First, though, it's important to remind ourselves *why* we're doing a budget. As we discussed, a budget is a mental-emotional exercise more than anything else; by doing a budget, we are putting ourselves in control of our money. But in addition to that, remember that we are trying to accomplish two specific financial goals:

1. Pay off all high-interest (10% or greater) debt.
2. Build an emergency fund equal to 6 months of expenses.

Let's go through these goals one at a time.

High-Interest Debt

For the purposes of this book, I define high-interest debt as any debt with an interest rate of 10% or greater. This will typically be things like credit cards and personal loans. These are what I call "bad" debts, primarily because you will end up paying far more in interest monthly than towards principal. You also typically can't leverage these debts to create new sources of income, which we'll discuss in more detail in Chapter 8. In other words, debt like this is wasted money, and the longer you sit on it, the more the interest builds.

Another reason we need to pay off our high-interest debt before moving on to the next step is that the monthly payments on high-interest debt typically consume an egregious amount of our income. If you are paying $200 a month in credit card interest, that's $200 being eaten out of your investable income, and it's serving you no productive purpose. If you can pay off high-interest debt, you'll immediately free up resources.

As for debts with lower interest rates, like student loans and mortgages, we're not worried about them at this stage because you can easily make enough money to outpace the interest on these loans through smart investing elsewhere. Eventually you will want to pay these off so that you can increase your overall net worth, but that should not be your primary focus at this stage.

Emergency Fund

An emergency fund is essential because it allows you to weather the ups and downs life throws at you. No matter how meticulously you budget, not everything can be planned for—car breakdowns, medical emergencies, layoffs, etc. If you have an emergency fund that can cover 6 months' worth of everyday expenses, you can survive most crises without having to dip into your long-term savings or disrupt your active investments. If you work hard to pay off all your high-interest debt and then launch into investing without building an emergency fund, what happens if someone runs a red light and totals your car? Your only choice will be to take out credit to cover the crisis, and now you're back where you started.

An emergency fund must be liquid assets, meaning you can access them easily and cost-free. Most likely this is a simple savings account. An IRA is not an emergency fund because you will pay penalties to access it, and nonliquid assets like real estate are not suitable emergency plans either. Emergency funds need to be quickly accessible, and you should not have to cash in bonds or CDs, sell stocks, or move assets to get the money when you need it.

Living Below Your Means

To accomplish both of these goals, we need to take *all* of our extra monthly income after expenses and put it either towards a debt or into the emergency fund. My personal recommendation is to focus on the emergency fund first, so that if there were to be a crisis while you were working on paying off your high-interest debt, you wouldn't have to resort to using a credit card. But however you decide to prioritize it, both of those goals *must* be completed before you can move on to Step 2.

Of course, our next obvious challenge is to generate a monthly surplus that we can divert to these goals. That's where the budget comes in. This is where we need to apply the age-old adage "live below your means." It's time to either lower your monthly expenses and/or raise your monthly income so that you can generate more excess income to apply to your goals.

To put this in perspective, take a moment to calculate the total amount of high-interest debt you need to pay off (use your liabilities details from the net worth section of the MPS) and the total amount you'd need in an emergency fund to cover 6 months of expenses (use your current expenses based on your first draft of your budget—you can always adjust the amount later if your expenses change). Add those two numbers. That is approximately the amount of money you will need to raise to accomplish your goals.

Now ask yourself, how quickly do you want to accomplish these goals? Are you going to take five years to complete these tasks, or are you willing and motivated to get it done in a year so you can move on? Approximately how much surplus income would you need each month to raise that amount of money in that timeframe?

With those numbers in mind, look at the total amount of surplus (investable) income you calculated with your budget. The difference tells you how much extra money you need to generate each month. Here's an example:

- Joe has $3,000 in credit card debt.
- His average monthly expenses are $1,200. This means he needs an emergency fund of approximately $7,000.

- Joe needs $10,000 to advance to Step 2.
- Joe wants to move on to Step 2 in a year. This means Joe needs approximately $833 each month in surplus income.
- Joe's current surplus income is $200/month. That means he needs to generate $633 more.

The reason I ask you to do all those calculations is so that you can get clear numbers written down on paper. It's one thing to go through your budget and cut $30 worth of subscription services, but if you are trying to generate $633/month in surplus income, you're going to have to dig deeper.

There are two major ways to generate more surplus income each month: Increase your earnings, or lower your expenses. Take another look at your budget sheet. Is your biggest problem that you make too little money? Or is reducing your expenses more critical?

Most people end up pursuing a combination of lowering their expenses and increasing their income. In the next chapter, we'll discuss in detail possible ways to raise your income, as this is crucial to moving beyond Step 2. If this is something you need to do, I encourage you to go ahead and read that chapter before making any major decisions. In the meantime, let's discuss some possible ways to reduce our expenses.

As we've mentioned, there are dozens of philosophies on how to manage your monthly expenses and stick to a budget—everything from skipping your daily Starbucks to using an envelope system to downtrading your car. Below are my top five pieces of advice for managing your expenses, but I highly encourage you to explore all the options available to you. Read some books on budgeting or subscribe to a money management podcast. Get yourself thinking daily about how to use your money more efficiently. Remember, the most important part about this process is the healthy habits you're developing. The money you save is important, yes, but even more valuable is the fact that you are now becoming *conscious* of your money and how you're using it. It's that self-awareness that will soon pay dividends.

Five Strategies for Managing Expenses

Prioritize. We talked about this earlier in the chapter, but it bears repeating: Prioritize your budget. Go through each line item and ask yourself, *"Does the amount of money I'm spending in this category reflect how important this item is to me?"* Having your priorities clearly in focus will not only make sure you're using your money most effectively; it will also help you feel more confident about the choices you make and give you the motivation necessary to stick to your limits.

Manage your emotions. This might sound like odd advice, but taking a few personality tests might actually jumpstart your financial progress. I recommend Money Club's Money Personality Quiz, which you can find at **Wealthtools.WorrytoWealthBook.com**, along with the other free resources accompanying this book. Remember that our financial "self" is deeply tied to our other "selves." If we are unhealthy in one "self," it will often manifest in all of our other "selves." This means that poor financial habits are often tied to emotional, mental, physical, or spiritual root causes.

Many people have developed unhealthy financial habits in an attempt to solve an undiagnosed core problem. Sadly, their financial influencers have often "helped" them create the makeshift systems that perpetuate the problem. Sometimes the correlations are obvious, like someone who uses "retail therapy" to stave off depression or self-loathing. But sometimes the issues are more subtle and deep-rooted, like a spouse that enables a partner to make poor financial decisions for fear of conflict or being abandoned.

If, during the course of this chapter, you've discovered some unhealthy financial habits in yourself, now's the time to dig deep and consider *why* you've been behaving that way. Is it simply a lack of self-control or a misunderstanding of money management? Or is there another cause? Involve mentors or counselors if necessary, and invest in the time needed to get yourself healed. Even if it costs you money, the small payment now could save you thousands moving forward.

Even if you're not trying to overcome a major psychological hurdle, understanding more about your personality type and how you relate with money will empower you to set healthy boundaries and make wise decisions. Remember, the most important factor for long term success is who we *become* out of this process, so take the time to get to know yourself.

Evaluate your large bills. Money management advice often focuses on the "little things" that can add up disastrously—streaming services, coffee runs, etc. And while it's critical that you manage the "small stuff," be careful not to overlook the "big stuff." The majority of our budget goes to six basic living expenses: housing, transportation, education, food, clothing, and health care. People often fail to consider these categories when looking for ways to reduce their expenses because these categories are "necessities." But just because a category is necessary doesn't mean you can't manage the cost.

Here are some questions to consider when evaluating your large bills:

- Is your house bigger than you need?
- Is your car more expensive than you need?
- Are you spending more than necessary on food (including trips to bars and restaurants)?
- Is your college education budget bigger than you need?

Some of these are easy to evaluate; for example, it's relatively easy to set a new monthly food budget and use a cash envelope system to stick with it. But some of these categories are more difficult to evaluate and may require a significant lifestyle change. Selling your home or car is a big decision and may not be easy. But if making the move could save you $500-$1,000 or more a month, you could greatly transform your financial situation and set you and your family on the track to possessing long-term, stable wealth, all without working any harder or longer.

For example, a woman once came to me for financial advice, claiming she was broke and had bad credit. I came to find out that she drove a $60k Audi and wore $400 Gucci belts every day. Simply downtrading her car and consigning half her closet would have changed her financial situation overnight. Was it worth the temporary glory of driving an Audi to be broke and never able to retire?

Remember, if you stick with this plan, you'll one day be able to afford your dream car and designer clothing. I am not saying that you can never have nice things. I am saying that if you sacrifice a short-term pleasure for the long-term gain, you can have all that and more, and you won't have to take on debt and ruin your credit score to get it.

Be flexible. Life isn't perfect. No matter how pristine your budget is, things are going to come up that you can't account for. While your emergency fund is there to swallow major crises, you don't want to have to tap into your emergency fund (or worse, your investable income) just because you forgot about your niece's birthday. Furthermore, while I'm strongly encouraging you to accept short-term pain for the long-term gain, I'm not saying that you can't *ever* get a coffee at Starbucks.

The solution is to factor a little bit of wiggle room into your budget. Many people accomplish this by adding a catch-all miscellaneous expense category as a line item. This shouldn't be a lot of money, perhaps $100 a month for a small family, but it will allow you to absorb small unexpected expenses like birthdays or buying a pizza because you had to work late. Having this cushion means that even if your month doesn't go perfectly, you're still on track. In addition, it helps avoid the shame and negative self-talk that kicks in when we slip up.

Invest first, spend second. Let me be clear: Your main goal during Step 1 is to pay off high-interest debt and build an emergency fund. The majority of your surplus income should be going to those goals. Now is not the time to dive headfirst into an asset strategy, such as snatching up real estate or investing in a private company.

However, remember why we're doing this. We're getting out of debt and building an emergency fund so that we can ultimately build wealth. Once those two goals are completed, we'll be diverting all that surplus income into investments. As we'll discuss in the next chapter, our next milestone will be to generate $1,600 per month in investable income.

If you have only been putting a little bit of money in an IRA or 401k—or perhaps not investing at all—that's a huge lifestyle change. Investment can no longer be an afterthought, a line item to tuck into your budget and divert a measly $100 into. It has to be a priority. Investment has to come first. In a way, it should even come before your regular monthly bills.

This doesn't mean that you skip a house payment to put that money in stocks, of course. But it does mean that all of your spending has to fall under the priority of having investable income.

This mental shift requires discipline and practice. That's why I strongly recommend that you immediately add a line item to your budget and put $100 a month in a stable public security. (We'll explain securities in more detail in Chapter 7.)

$100/month isn't enough to get us to our goal of one million, nor is it enough to retire on. The purpose of this is to develop a habit. By getting into the habit of investing before spending, even if it's only $100, you're exercising the financial "muscles" you'll need when we start dealing with bigger numbers. The self-discipline that $100/month will earn for you far outweighs the temporal value of anything else you could have purchased with that money.

Time Well Spent

While we've spent most of Step 1 focusing on controlling our money, there's another resource of even greater value that we need to manage: Time.

We'll discuss time extensively in Chapter 9. Time is the integral, often unspoken factor in all successful investment strategies; it is the variable that will multiply every dollar you save. But while many people understand the concept of time in compounding interest, many fail to examine how they are spending time every day.

When you think about it, we truly do "spend" time. Each day is just like a budget: We receive 24 hours—that's 1,440 minutes or 86,400 seconds—and we decide what each minute will be invested into. However, our time "budgets" differ from our money budgets in one drastic way: **We can always earn more money, but we can never earn more time!** For each minute we have, we can either spend it, waste it, or invest it, but we cannot save it. This is why I truly believe time is more valuable than money.

In my experience, many people who are in the Worry stage waste more time than money. Although this is absolutely not true for everyone, I have worked with so many people who complain about their lack of money and financial security, only to discover that the majority of their day is spent on *problem-escaping activities* rather than *goal-achieving actions*.

This is why it is so critical that we go through the same process of "budget reduction" with time that we do with money. The exact same principles apply:

- We start by tracking how we're currently using time each day.
- We evaluate our priorities and assign a value to each category.
- Then we adjust our schedule to match our priorities.

While we're in Step 1, our biggest priorities need to be **earning and learning.** We should be devoting the majority of our most valuable resource to either earning more money (which we're putting towards high-interest debts and our emergency fund; later, that money is invested) or educating ourselves with skills that build towards our future (more on that in the next section). This means the bulk of our day should be devoted to those two pursuits.

As you recall from the chart in Chapter 4, I recommend that someone in the Worry stage be spending 10 hours a day earning and 2 hours a day learning. Yes, I realize that's an obsessive schedule. Over the course of my life I have lost friends and angered students with this particular teaching, and I suspect I may have just lost some readers. I will freely admit that what I am recommending is a **temporary out-of-balance lifestyle**, and here's why I think that's essential.

Financial success is just like training for the Olympics or any other professional sport. Professional sports players don't just spend a few hours a week dabbling in their sport; they devote their lives to it. All of their resources are used to achieve that goal, and all of their decisions are made with the ultimate prize—a gold medal—in mind. When they choose to exercise, train, and adhere to a special diet, they are making those short-term sacrifices so they can have the long-term glory of being successful in their field.

Now you may be thinking, "I am not a professional athlete," but financial success has to be fought and won the same way. If you do not make financial success a big priority—both with your money *and* with your time—you will never be a "professional." This doesn't mean you need to become a real estate agent, mortgage broker, or day trader. In fact, as we'll discover in Chapter 7, you can probably leverage the activities you love most and use your natural skills to create wealth. But it does mean that your financial progress needs to come first, and that involves devoting the best of your time and energy to earning money and educating yourself.

This lifestyle will not make you popular. I should know. As I mentioned when I told you my personal story, between the ages of 18-21 I was particularly obsessed with learning anything I could get my hands on, especially about financial literacy and personal development. I irritated many people with my incessant ravings about what I was learning, and I suspect I lost more than a few friends because of it. But as we'll learn soon, time is an essential ingredient of long-term wealth creation, and the more you can invest early on, the greater your financial return will be later. If you sacrifice now, you'll actually be able to work *less* hours over the total span of your life.

I understand that scheduling is not an exact science, and everyone's situation is different. If you're actively in college, you'll probably end up spending more hours learning than earning. On the other hand, if you decide to take out a temporary second job to knock out your credit card debt, you may emphasize earning more than learning for the first year or two. That's okay, but I must strongly encourage you to make sure you're both learning *and* earning, even if your ratios are slightly different. That's because you need to be developing both of those skills simultaneously to be prepared for Step 2.

For example, if you chose only to work and never learn, you might be able to pay off your debt very quickly, but when you get to the end you might realize that you haven't developed any financial skills to prepare you to handle the investable income you suddenly have. On the flip side, if you chose to only learn while you're at college and not earn, you might graduate with only a piece of paper and a crushing amount of student debt, having no practical experience or cash savings to get you started on your new career. Make it a priority to earn, even if it's just a part-time job or an employment opportunity at your college. I promise you it will be time well-spent.

Beginning Your Self-Guided Education

Once you've set aside that time to learn, the question becomes: What should you be studying?

At the Worry stage, the answer is really **anything and everything that will increase your knowledge base in an intentional way.** While financial education and self-improvement should always be at the top of your list, now is the time to read any book you can get your hands on, listen to podcasts by well-respected industry leaders, and sample a variety of topics. This is especially true if you haven't decided on a career path yet, or if you're unsure what your long-term asset strategy will be. Skim Chapter 7 to get a feel for the variety of investment opportunities available, pick a few that strike you, and find some books or seminars on each one. Get a taste and see what appeals to your interests and competencies.

If you're already settled in a career path or have a strong idea of what your interests and competencies are, submerge yourself in your industry. Find the experts in your field and read their books or follow their podcasts. Ask yourself, *"What is the next step in education that would allow me to graduate to the next level in my field?"* Start tracking down the resources that you need and study them.

Additionally, of course, your "diet" should include a hearty helping of financial education. I strongly recommend Hill's *Think and Grow Rich* be at the top of your list. Here are a few other suggestions: *How to Win Friends and Influence People* by Dale Carnegie, *The Richest Man in Babylon* by

George Samuel Clason, *The E-Myth* by Michael E. Gerber, and *The Magic of Thinking Big* by David J. Schwartz.

Lastly, I strongly encourage you to include psychology and self-help in your repertoire. Anything you can learn about yourself—and other people—will empower you to better manage your money and time. Remember, we are *becoming* someone as we're taking this financial journey, and personal growth is always a good investment.

Moving into Step 2

Before you move into Step 2, you *must* have:

1. Paid off all high-interest (10% or greater) debt.
2. Built an emergency fund equivalent to 6 months of expenses.
3. Adjusted your schedule to prioritize both earning and learning.

Once you've completed those goals, you might find that you're still in the Worry stage based on net worth. That's okay. As long as you're following a budget and have your high-interest debts and emergency fund secured, you're ready to focus on Step 2: Generating Investable Income.

CASE STUDY #3

Alexandra C., Washington, D.C.

Alexandra's path to wealth is a true incarnation of the American dream. She grew up in a very financially unstable household in a low-income neighborhood in Brazil. After receiving an undergrad in biochemistry at a university in Brazil, she moved to the US with just a suitcase of clothes, $250 in cash, and a 1st grade comprehension of the English language. However, she had discipline and determination by the truckloads.

As you'll see, Alexandra's path follows two core principles:

1. She never stopped investing in her own education, and

2. She consistently kept her living expenses low to save as much as possible.

After moving to the US, Alexandra began by working at a lab in California while continuing to learn English. By the age of 31, she had received a PhD in molecular biology from Texas A&M; she then went on to do her post-doc training at Hopkins in Baltimore. Three years later, she left the academic science track and switched to a job in the private sector with a starting salary of $50,000. By age 38, she had received an MBA in organizational behavior and moved from working in research and development to operations and management, thereby increasing her salary by providing unique value that few people in her company could supply.

By age 43, she had finished paying off her house and continued to invest aggressively into her 401k. At age 54, she was promoted to an executive position and became eligible to defer her salary, which allowed her to reduce her tax liability and invest even more in public stocks. She was able to take advantage of this unique opportunity because she had proactively saved throughout her entire life, and her car, house, and kids' college expenses were already paid in full. Furthermore, when her salary increased, she did not increase her spending and lifestyle; she only increased her saving and investing.

Finally, she retired at age 59. She currently lives solely off the interest earned from her deferred salary, about $60k/year. She spends most of her time gardening, volunteering, and working towards a new degree in theology. She still has not increased her lifestyle, and because of that her net worth is currently an impressive $4.5 million.

In summary, Alexandra used her career in science, operations, and leadership to generate a high income (vA) to invest aggressively in public stocks (vB) to grow her net worth through compounding over time (vD). Then, when she reached a certain point in her career, she was able to employ leverage (vC) to defer her salary for stock options and ultimately multiply her net worth greatly.

Alexandra's path to wealth didn't involve buying tons of properties, scoring big on investments, or starting a new business. She simply mastered the fundamentals: keep learning to become more valuable, keep expenses modest, and save/invest aggressively.

When I asked her what were the most important lessons she learned along the way, she shared the following:

1. "Never stop learning. The workplace is advancing so fast that if you aren't growing with it, you're moving backwards. Once I realized that education was my

way out of poverty, I also realized that it was going to be my way to wealth.

2. "Your future will become your present. Taking the long view of life helped me stay disciplined to keep working and saving hard. I saw my parents spin their wheels for decades because they didn't have the discipline to save. You can't predict the future, but you can influence it.

3. "Emotional intelligence is more important than intellect. When you live with respect and integrity, people want to help you. When you take a genuine interest in helping them, they want to help you more. Not only is growing with other people more beneficial financially, it also makes the journey much more fulfilling in ways beyond just the money.

4. "Find purpose in deeper things. You need financial stability, but you don't need to spend money on expensive possessions or activities to be happy. Find a deeper meaning to your life that doesn't require lavish spending to fulfill."

The primary solution to all your financial crises lies within your ability to generate enough investable income.

SIX

Step 2: Generate Investable Income

I'm not going to beat around the bush with this one. Our goal in Step 2 is very straightforward: **We need to find manageable, long-term ways to generate $1,600 a month ($20,000 a year) in investable income.**

We've mentioned this figure before, so some of you are probably asking: Why is $20,000 a year the magic number? Because investing $20,000 a year over fifteen years will equal $300,000 of contributed asset value, and by using principles of leverage (vC) and time (vD), which we'll discuss in Chapters 8 and 9, you can reliably transform $300,000 into one million.

Of course, because the wealth creation formula is made of fluid variables, you *could* reach one million with less investable income if you were willing to compensate in another area. But our goal here is not to discuss all the *possible* ways to reach one million—it's to focus on the most *reliable* and *efficient* ways for the average household to grow their net worth. Based on my nearly four decades of experience, I've found that $20,000 a year is a sustainable, reasonable amount that will allow most families to reach their goals within twenty years. So, until time and experience reveal a different path to you, let's assume for the moment that $20,000 a year is your ideal goal.

For many of you, that number is probably very daunting. Depending on the results you got using the Money Positioning System in Chapter 4, you may have started this journey with almost no investable income. Many people in this financial stage don't make that much at their day job, so the idea of coming up with an *extra* $1,600 each month seems downright impossible.

Stay with me and don't lose hope yet. If you've been applying the principles in this book thus far, you've already accomplished some significant financial goals and made more progress than many people will in their lifetime. That same level of focus, determination, and ingenuity can get you through Step 2 as well, so keep your eye on the prize.

Some of you might be thinking that $1,600 a month is a rather extravagant number, and you'd be right. Remember, we're aiming for a rather extravagant goal; having one million dollars in net worth within twenty years will put you in the top 15% nationwide in terms of net worth[5]. You could invest less, but that would leave you with less later on. This is another example of temporarily adopting an out-of-balance lifestyle for the long-term gain; by making it a priority to invest a large amount of money early, you will reap greater dividends later.

For that same reason, I strongly encourage you to strictly stick to the goal of $1,600/month, even if you think you can achieve your goal on less. When we explored the wealth creation formula in Chapter 3, we noted that, because it's an equation of variables, there are an endless number of combinations that will yield the same result of increased net worth. It is very possible to invest less per month and make up the difference with one of the other variables. However, unless you're jumpstarting your wealth building through a profitable sale or another major asset event like an inheritance, the variable that usually has to pick up the slack is time. In almost all cases, if you invest less (both in money and in daily time), you will end up needing more time over the long term to reach your goals.

It's important to remember that this is a *temporary* lifestyle. In this chapter we're going to focus on active ways to

---

[5] Based on 2019 numbers. https://www.federalreserve.gov/publications/files/scf20.pdf

increase your income, most likely through adjusting your job prospects. For your first few years of wealth building, the majority of your investable income will probably be earned through your direct effort. But as soon as you transition into Step 3 and begin to build your long-term asset strategy, your money will begin to make more money through interest, business profits, rent payments, and other passive means. If you remain structured and focused and invest wisely, soon your passive income will give you all the investable surplus you need to keep building. That's when you'll transition into the higher stages of wealth creation and begin to spend less time earning.

Keep this in mind as we explore some of the possible options for increasing your income during Step 2; just because you commit to work a part-time job for a year, for example, doesn't mean you're committing to that lifestyle for the rest of your life.

We also should remember that the habits and character traits we develop are just as important as the money we earn, if not more so. Even if you could build wealth through another combination of the variables, the exercise of dedicating that much investable income per month is invaluable. So even if you only have to stick with it for a year before other variables and asset drivers kick in, make investable income your priority. As long as you keep putting it on the backburner, both financially and mentally-emotionally, you are subconsciously telling yourself that wealth creation is merely an afterthought in your life.

The Truth About Investable Income

Before we go on, let's remind ourselves what "investable income" really means. Investable income is *any* surplus income after expenses. This means that investable income is not a line item in your budget; rather, *all* of your income that's not allocated to another budget item goes towards investing.

We discussed this briefly in the previous chapter, but I want to emphasize this again: This is a massive mindset shift. At a primal level, you have to start thinking about your income as a driver towards wealth. You are not budgeting for wealth creation like you budget for food, clothing, and healthcare. You make income to build wealth, and your household expenses are just part of your overhead. In other words, you're **investing first, spending second.**

This means, of course, that one of the ways to increase your monthly investable income is to lower your expenses. Much like a business saving on its operating expenses, any amount of money you save on your monthly expenses means more investable income for you and your family. We discussed this in depth in the previous chapter, so we're not going to get into the mechanics of budget reduction here. But it bears repeating, because some of you might be able to get to $1,600/month in investable income purely by adjusting your expenses.

Most people are going to have to pursue a combination of increasing their income and reducing expenses, but it makes sense to explore all your options before making a lifestyle change. If you had to pick between picking up a second job and sacrificing your vacation budget, which would you choose? These are the questions you should ask yourself.

Giving Yourself a Raise

After the option of lowering expenses has been explored, we need to move on to the next obvious way of generating more investable income: increasing how much we earn per month.

Many people balk when I mention earning more money. Perhaps many of you reading this book can identify with these feelings: You already feel like you work so hard and spend so much of your time thinking about money in some way. This is especially true if you're in the Worry stage; even when you're not at work, much of your week is consumed worrying about money or dealing with money-related stresses.

Hopefully all the preparation we did in Step 1—gaining control of our finances through budgeting, paying off high-interest debt, and building an emergency fund—has alleviated some of that immediate stress. But even so, the thought of striving to earn more—especially $1,600 more—might still daunt and upset you.

However, if we *effectively* and *wisely* apply the income variable to our lives, in the end we shouldn't have to "strive" at all. It doesn't mean that we won't have to work hard, and it doesn't mean that we won't have to sacrifice in the short-term. But solving the income variable is *not* about running out to get 3 part time jobs and working 24/7 just so you have money to buy stock. Step 2 is about making more money, yes, but it's also about finding the *best* way for *you* to make more money based on your unique situation, skills, network, and resources.

For example, picking up an extra job might be a great short-term solution for a single young person or a college student. If you recall from my story, I temporarily continued to work for minimum wage at an athletic club while I studied real estate and grew my mortgage lending business.

But on the contrary, if you're a small business owner, picking up a second job would probably be an inefficient use of time. A far wiser course of action would be for you to devote all of your productive energy into growing your business, which would not only increase your income but also increase your net worth by raising the value of your company. In this case, taking on a second job that's outside of your line of work would be a distraction and might even hinder your financial progress in the long run.

This is why, even though our emphasis in Step 2 is on increasing our investable income, you must remember the path that gives you the biggest *immediate* raise isn't always the *best* option. In the case of the small business owner, getting a second job would give them an immediate boost in income, but investing in building up their business could earn them more in the long run.

Another example of this trade-off is investing in more education. An investment in education needs to be critically analyzed like any other financial investment, but it may lead to a much greater increase in income than a temporary evening job.

When considering any possible income solution, ask yourself: "What will this prospect do for me in three, five, and ten years?" Compare that with your overall goals. That will give you a pretty solid idea of whether or not that particular solution supports your core priorities.

This is also why in Step 1 we taught ourselves to critically evaluate our use of time. If you are squandering time on non-earning activities or grinding away at an ill-fitting job, you may be making yourself busy and exhausted without actually having a profit to show for it. When evaluating your income, make sure to ask yourself difficult questions about not only what you do *at* work but also what you do when you're off duty. On one hand, redeeming time from an unprofitable activity might free up energy to work more hours. On the other, you may find that some of the time you've spent "working" and "earning" is actually costing you money in the long run.

The most efficient income strategy is going to be different for every person, and it will change constantly as you go through different seasons of your life and your economic outlook shifts. New opportunities, changes at work, and other factors can cause your income drivers to change over time. This is why it is vitally important to complete the Your Way to $20k self-assessment from Chapter 4, so that you can understand where your strengths lie, as well as make an honest assessment of the earning potential of your various income options.

In the next section I'm going to walk you through the finances of a fictional couple. I'm going to show you their income and expenses and suggest a variety of ways they could increase their monthly investable income. After that, I have a list of additional income-generating options for you to consider. This list is by no means exhaustive, and no one option is necessarily better than any others. My intent is to help you think outside the box when it comes to income, and to encourage that you ask the right questions, which will enable you to discover the best income driver for your situation.

The Example of John and Mary

John is a middle school math teacher making $48,000 per year. He is married to Mary, who is also an English teacher at the elementary school level and makes $55,000 per year. Both are 31 years old and have been teaching for 8 years. John has a bachelor's degree and his wife Mary has a master's degree. They have one child who is five years old, and they have the financial profile described below.

- **Gross household income: $103,000**
- Taxes: $30,000 per year (29% of gross)
- Net (after taxes) household income: $73,000
- Hypothetical household annual expenses: (% of gross income)
    - Mortgage: $25,000 a year (24%)
    - Auto payment: $7,200 (7%)
    - Health insurance: $5,600 (5%)
    - Auto/life/disability insurance: $2,500 (2%)
    - Food: $9,000 (9%)
    - Clothing: $4,800 (5%)
    - Gas/auto repair: $3,000 (3%)
    - Dining/entertainment: $4,800 (5%)

- Education/sports/travel: $3,000 (3%)
- Miscellaneous: $4,000 (4%)
- Retirement plan: $4,000 (4%)
- **Total expenditures: $68,900 or 100% of net income**
- **Investable Income: $4,000 (retirement plan)**

John and Mary aren't doing too badly on the income scale; their income is very close to the mean family income and nearly double the median by 2019 economic numbers[6]. And yet, based on their expenditures, which are typical of the average family, they will have a very difficult time generating $20,000 a year in investable income without making some major changes.

Here are some options that John and Mary could consider. What is your opinion of each option? What are the pros and cons of each? If you were in their situation, which option(s) would you choose?

- John could go back to school to get his master's degree, which would result in a $8,000 annual raise. However, they would have to incur $30,000 in education costs to obtain the degree.
- Either or both could consider a completely new career path that would earn them higher salaries. However,

---

[6] https://www.federalreserve.gov/publications/files/scf20.pdf

their degrees might become useless, and they would both have to sacrifice their love of teaching children.
- John has discovered a separate income opportunity. Because he is good with math, he could take on a part-time finance job where he can work about 12 hours a week (8 during the week and 4 on weekends) and make about $15,000 a year.
- Mary could also coach the high school track team for an extra $4,000 a year. Additionally, there is a commissioned position available within the school district that would earn her another $10,000 a year.
- Either John or Mary could start their own math tutoring or private coaching business and earn an extra $16,000, possibly more, per year. However, they may have to invest in education to learn how to run a business, and there might be start-up costs involved.
- John and Mary could lower their household expenses.

If you were in John and Mary's situation, what would you choose? Are there any other income solutions that you could add to the list?

5 Other Potential Income Drivers

Hopefully the above example showed you how, in any given situation, there are multiple ways to generate more investable income. Many people employ a combination of several options, and a little bit of creativity can uncover some effective (and even fun) ways to earn more money—many of which don't involve changing your career path. Here are five things to consider when solving your income variable.

Be more valuable. Can you increase your value as an employee at your current job in a way that will earn you higher wages? Would any additional education or training be required? What are the costs associated with that extra training? In general, look at the upward mobility potential in your current line of work. Can you be promoted? What would you need to do to earn this promotion? What would your income be if you got that promotion?

Work a part-time job within your field. When considering taking on a second job, McDonald's isn't your only option. Are there part-time job opportunities within your field, perhaps even at your current place of employment? If you can stay within your field, you may be able to use your additional training to increase your value and eventually move into a higher position, eliminating the need for a second job.

Work a part-time job outside of your field. For some people, getting a second job is the best solution. If this is a viable option for you, look for part-time jobs that would either increase your quality of life or teach you a new skill that you could use to drive profits later. For example, if your day job is construction but you really love kids, working part time at a school or daycare would be a way to increase your income while fulfilling yourself as a person. On the other hand, if you're in construction but can pick up a part-time job that will teach you accounting or business skills, you could be giving yourself the tools needed to start your own construction business one day.

Learn a new, more profitable skill while maintaining the day job. In other words, pay your way through college, even if "college" is entirely made up of self-education. For example, one of the editors who helped me with this book cleans houses by day to pay her regular expenses while doing freelance editing on nights and weekends. All of her freelance income goes towards accomplishing her Steps 1 and 2 goals, and at the same time she's building a business that will one day be more profitable than housecleaning.

Focus on commission and profits rather than wages. As we'll learn in Chapter 8, wages are a form of leverage. Consider the previous example of a housecleaner: If her employer pays her $12/hour to clean houses but charges the customer $30/hour for the service, her employer has just leveraged her labor to make an $18/hour profit, excluding other expenses. This is one reason why the earning potential of most wage-based jobs is limited. If you feel like your upward mobility is limited at your current job, you should strongly consider shifting your focus towards a position that earns you commissions (such as sales or independent contractor work) or puts you in a position to receive profits (such as from a business you own or have a stake in).

One thing you'll notice about my personal finance journey is that I quickly got myself into a position where I was earning commission. If I had simply been working Ron's leads for a fixed hourly wage, I would not have been able to exponentially increase my income.

Shifting your main income driver to commissions or profits may involve changing jobs or careers, but you might also find that there are commissioned opportunities within your current line of work. Your current employer may even have a commissioned role that you can perform in addition to your main position. Either way, it's worth the time to do your research and ask questions about the options available to you.

The 50/50 Split

Building your investable income is a process. Some of you may have already had incomes high enough to conquer this step; some of you might get there in a few short months with some creative budgeting or a new side job. But for most of you, it is going to take several months, perhaps even a year or two, to build your income to the point where you're investing $1,600 a month. That's okay, as long as you commit to getting started immediately.

I hope I prove to you over the course of this book that this investment is not only absolutely critical but also immensely valuable. But the question then becomes: What should you be doing with your investable income in the meantime? As you're growing your monthly investable income and developing a long-term asset strategy, what should you be doing with the amount you have right now?

I strongly encourage you to split your monthly investable income and put half in stable public securities, like a retirement fund, and half in a savings account. I would advise this regardless of the amount of money you currently have per month. If your monthly investable income is $200, put $100 in savings and $100 in public securities. If your monthly investable income is $1,000, put $500 in savings and $500 in public securities.

I recommend this strategy for several reasons. First, putting half of your investable income in public securities allows you to immediately put time and compounding interest to work for you. Again, we'll delve into public securities and how to best utilize them in the next chapter, but the interest earned on them will allow your money to outrun inflation, enabling your net worth to grow over time.

Second, putting half of your investable income in savings allows you to build a liquid, easily accessible nest egg that you can tap into when you start Step 3. This nest egg gives you a financial safety net—in addition to your 6-month emergency fund—empowering you to take risks, which is essential for many of the asset strategies we'll explore in Step 3. This nest egg also gives you cash that you can use to purchase assets.

You don't want to get to Step 3 and find that you have to cash out your retirement fund to buy your first asset. On the other hand, you don't want to put all of your investable income in a savings account that earns little to no interest, because that money will only lose value the longer you sit on it. This is why I recommend splitting your investable income half and half as long as you're in Step 2.

As you near the end of Step 2 and generate more and more investable income, you might be tempted to dive into some of the asset strategies we'll discuss in the next chapter. While there's no hard and fast rules with wealth creation, I implore you to be patient and not rush into a new asset strategy too soon.

There are several reasons for this. First, you may not yet have the financial resources to weather the risks associated with some assets. Jumping into a speculative or fluctuating asset strategy at this point could leave you suffering if the market downturns, which might mean you have to dip into savings, take out debt, or use some of your investable income to fix the problem. All of these will put you behind on your goals and increase the time it takes to graduate to Step 3.

Second, you might not yet be ready to fully leverage debt. Many of the asset strategies we'll discuss involve various forms of leverage, such as borrowing against stock to purchase more stock, or loaning money out on interest. Debt always comes with risks, and if you have not yet built up the financial reserve to handle those risks, one bad deal could be a huge setback in your financial progress.

Third, you want to take the time to fully educate yourself on all the available asset strategies. Not only do you want to be sure you pick a strategy that's a good fit for you, but you also want to make sure you thoroughly understand the vehicle you'll be using to generate wealth. For all asset strategies to be effective, they need to be used wisely. That means understanding the risks, being knowledgeable about the market, and knowing how to leverage the unique characteristics of your field. You don't want to commit to being a landlord only to find out that you absolutely detest every minute of it. You don't want to invest in a franchise only to find out you have no idea how the corporate structure works. Nor do you want to throw your money aimlessly at miscellaneous strategies, hoping something will stick. Take the time to do your research, consult with your spouse and trusted financial mentors, and make a decision that's right for *you* and your family.

With that in mind, remember: You should still be spending around 10 hours a day earning and 2 hours a day learning at this stage. In Step 1, our earning time was spent generating money to pay off high-interest debt and build an emergency fund. As you move through Step 2, your earning time should become more purposeful. Your goal is not to do anything and everything just to scrounge up $1,600 dollars a month; your goal is to use the principles in this chapter to design a *long-term* method of generating sufficient investable income. Remember, you're going to want to maintain this level of investable income until your assets begin to generate income and grow on their own. Babysitting every night of the week is a great short-term income strategy for a short-term goal, but it's probably not sustainable, even for a single young person. So make sure your earning time is being invested into something that will serve your long-term purposes, whether that's growing a new business or moving up the corporate ladder.

Your learning time should also become more purposeful during this stage. You should still be feeding your mind with as much financial wisdom as possible, and you should continue to study psychology and self-help. But the main goal of your learning time is now to become an expert in the asset strategy (or strategies) that you're considering getting into. As soon as you reach that $1,600/month threshold, you're going to want to get invested into your long-term asset strategy as soon as you can. The more time you can spend educating yourself on that strategy now, the faster you can start making your money work for you when you get into Step 3.

That's why I would encourage you, even if you'll be working on Step 2 for some time, to go ahead and read the rest of the book. Pay special attention to Chapter 7 where we discuss some of the available asset options. Pick out the ones that appeal to you and find 2-3 books on each one. By the time you've read those books, you'll have a pretty good idea of whether or not that asset strategy is a good fit for your needs and personality.

Moving into Step 3

We only had one goal for Step 2: To generate $1,600/month in investable income. If you're at that level, you're ready to move on to Step 3, regardless of what stage you're in by net worth measurements. Most of you will have probably moved into the Foundation stage by now, and you should congratulate yourselves on making such amazing progress in such a short time. But even if you still have less than $50k in total net worth, that's okay. As long as you're generating

$1,600/month in investable income, and you paid off all your high-interest debt and built a 6-month emergency fund in Step 1, you're ready to move on. It's time to take the leap and put your hard-earned money to work.

CASE STUDY #4

Alex F., Amelia Island, FL

Alex is one of a kind. He was 42 years old at the time of the interview. He cited his parents as being one of the few positive financial influencers he had while growing up. He attended high-school and managed to get straight C grades, but he failed to secure any college degree and was ultimately kicked out of school. Despite these seeming disadvantages, Alex has still managed to build an astonishing net worth of *twelve million dollars*—and counting!

At the time of the interview, he was a partner in a private equity firm. When I asked him about his average income over the past three years, he responded: "$600k, and $400k is from passive income." He, too, did not inherit any of his wealth.

He worked multiple jobs during his early years as well, with his first job being part-time at the help desk of an I.T.

firm for three years. His second job was as a computer manager for a non-profit company. His third job was with Boeing as an I.T. manager. His fourth job was at Lockheed Martin as a systems engineer, where he was later promoted to engineering manager. He explained that he was earning high incomes by his mid-to-late 20s.

After he left his fourth job, Alex worked for himself and started a few businesses as a builder and mortgage lender. He became self-employed at the age of 27. He always felt like he could do things better working for himself, so becoming self-employed was a clear strategy for him.

He thrived by creating his income variable (vA) solution early on in his life through multiple well-paying jobs. At age 12 he had the lucrative job of cutting grass; he continued to work at an I.T. company through high school; and then by age 20 he was making $40k a year. He was able to generate solid income through salaries before transferring his attention to building his own businesses.

He started a title business, then a construction business, and then a mortgage business. Much of his investable income came from the profits of the mortgage company over a 4-year time span. Here is a table illustrating the extraordinary way his investable income grew over time:

Alex's Age	Annual Investable Income
20-30	$100k
30-40	$500k

Alex did not go crazy with his investments to create a complex vB solution. Instead, he kept it simple. Much of his net worth was created from his self-employment and business investment, while about 25% came from real estate investments.

When I asked him to encourage the younger generation towards wealth creation, he responded:

- Only seek a path to wealth if it is going to bring you joy. *Only* do what you love.
- Always spend less money than you make.
- Only purchase things that you absolutely need.
- Focus on building a great company and not on personal enrichment.

When asked what three major attributes contributed to his wealth, Alex had this to say:

- Most people do not focus when they are in their 20s and early 30s to generate income and invest early enough.
- Save and invest as early as possible.

- Always live below your means.

In summary, Alex utilized his focus and skills to generate a high-income solution (vA). 75% of his net worth was created through self-employed earnings. He then solved the variable vB by buying real estate and selling a business.

If there was one sure way towards wealth creation, it is through acquiring assets.

SEVEN

Step 3: Discover Your Asset Strategy

Like Step 2, our goal in Step 3 is fairly straightforward: **We need to discover the long-term asset strategy that works best for you and your family so you can pour your investable income into a vehicle that will make your money grow.**

But, like we discovered with income drivers in the last chapter, you don't want to throw money sporadically at random investment opportunities and hope something sticks. You need to hone in on the strategy that is most effective for you individually, which means being intimately familiar with your strengths, limitations, interests, and competencies, as well as being honest with yourself about the active time and energy you have to commit.

I'll be honest with you: This isn't going to happen overnight. Don't expect to read this chapter and come away with a 100% clear and confident idea of what you want to do with your money.

Why? Well, first, there's simply not enough space in this book to thoroughly explore even half of the asset options available to you. This chapter is the financial equivalent of a career fair at a college; I'm going to show you a sampling of what's out there and give you my best recommendations, but you'll need to learn more to discover the best asset strategy for your unique situation.

I hope that, as you go through this process, you continue to study psychology and self-help, take personality and career assessments, and involve trusted mentors, counselors, and your spouse, if applicable. You are determining the future of your money and making a choice about what *you* want to invest yourself into. No one else gets to make that choice for you.

That said, don't let the sheer volume of choices disturb you. Remember, you don't have to put all your money into one vehicle (in fact, you shouldn't), and your portfolio will continue to shift over time. You can always try something new down the road. You also should continually remind yourself that it's okay to make mistakes. There's no shame in trying a method and failing as long as you course-correct and keep going. This is coming from the guy who lost over six million in one unfortunate incident. If I can pick myself back up after that devastating mistake, you can brush yourself off and try something new when an investment strategy doesn't go your way.

With that in mind, let's take a tour of the world of assets and see if we can find the vehicle that's right for you.

Demystifying Asset Acquisition

Asset acquisition: It's an uppity-sounding phrase you've probably heard thrown around by people who appear to have way more money than you do. For many who are just moving out of the Worry stage, "assets" sound like something bankers, mortgage lenders, and day traders have. It can sound scary, complicated, and *way* too expensive for your fledgling budget.

This is why many people fail to develop effective asset strategies and instead just let their money sit in stagnant bank accounts (if they save at all). Some believe they can't afford assets, so they never try and they never invest the time to educate themselves. Others get swept up in the glamorized version of Wall Street they see on TV and unwisely throw their money into speculative, ill-managed strategies. Others fail to study their core competencies and just jump into whatever asset strategy they think they're "supposed" to have—like buying real estate—often ending up in a field they hate and can't manage. All of these options lead to lost money and, usually, people pulling out of the game and failing to invest at all.

However, asset acquisition doesn't have to be complicated. The average American family—with two working parents, some rowdy kids, and a stack of monthly bills—can safely and effectively invest in assets. If you take the time to truly understand the purpose of asset acquisition and how it works, you can make your money work for you without "betting the farm" on a risky venture or having to complete a four-year degree in financial management.

First, let's remind ourselves what an asset is. An asset is simply an object that represents monetary value. Cash is an asset. Bank accounts are assets. Cars, real estate, and valuable objects like art and antiques can be assets. Stocks and businesses are assets.

That said, just because you paid money for something doesn't mean it's an asset. The items we purchase to consume—like food, clothing, and household furniture—are generally not assets. Once something is consumed (like food), it has no more monetary value, and most of the items in our home are not liquid enough to be converted into cash to invest elsewhere. Sure, you could sell your old record collection for a short burst of investable income—and if you've got significant debt and want to jumpstart your financial progress, you might consider doing that. But cleaning out your closet is not a long-term, sustainable strategy.

On the other hand, if you wanted to invest time into hunting garage sales for old records and reselling them online for their full value because you have the expertise and connections to do so, that can become a viable income driver. But even in that case, the records themselves are not really assets. The record-trading business you're developing, however, could be.

The line between income and asset drivers is often blurred, because assets should bring you income, and sources of income can become assets themselves. We'll discuss this more shortly, but I don't want you to get hung up on the distinction between your income (vA) solutions and your asset (vB) solutions. They should both be working together. What I do want you to be wary of, however, is deluding yourself into thinking that extravagant personal purchases are building your net worth. Very few of the items we acquire for ourselves count as assets.

This is why I generally don't include the value of a primary residence when calculating net worth, even though it is a piece of real estate that could be sold. The primary function of your home is to provide you with shelter, not a means of income. You'll still hear people encourage you to pay off the mortgage on your primary residence, but that's mainly to free up investable income and remove the liability of the mortgage. Consequently, the mortgage liability on your primary residence should be included in the assessment of your overall financial situation, but I do not consider it when calculating total net worth.

This brings up the next important point we want to remember. Net worth is calculated by subtracting the total value of our liabilities from the total value of our assets. Therefore, when we say our goal is to have a net worth of one million dollars, that means we want to possess a million dollars' worth of *debt-free* assets.

Debt is an important leveraging tool, and there are many ways to use it effectively. We'll discuss this more in the next chapter, but the reason I mention this now is because I want to remind you that buying a $60k Audi entirely on credit does *not* increase your net worth. Unless you have a plan to rent that Audi out like a limo and turn it into an income driver, you've just *subtracted* from your net worth instead of added to it. Keep this in mind as we look at the various asset strategies in this chapter. Some of them, like real estate, often involve leveraging debt in the beginning. But let's be clear: **all effective asset drivers should have a plan whereby they become debt-free in 10-20 years.**

Another thing to remember as you explore possible asset drivers is that you should *never* take anyone's word for it—even mine. Always do your own research before committing to an investment. That research should involve reading material from 2-3 different experts, none of which should be personal friends or family members. Just because an asset worked for someone else doesn't mean it will work for you, especially when so much is dependent on timing and the whim of the market. Your friend may have gotten rich on Bitcoin last week, but that doesn't mean you can jump in now and expect the same results. Be smart, and make sure your research is current.

By the same token, our asset portfolio should adhere to that ancient advice of "don't put all your eggs in one basket." Although everyone will have primary drivers that they put the bulk of their resources into, a healthy portfolio is always diversified. This is not only because having diversified options allows you to weather the risks of the market, but also because different assets are useful for different goals.

Remember how I advised you in Step 2 to split your investable income 50/50, putting half in public securities and half in savings? That was because those two assets serve different purposes. The savings account gives you liquid assets to invest, while the public securities increases the chances that your money to grow over time through compounding interest and market forces. The savings account is money you plan to withdraw in the near future; the public securities is money you plan to withdraw in the distant future.

The same principle applies to your asset portfolio. While all healthy assets should increase your net worth, they have different liquidity levels and serve different purposes in the short- and long-term. For example, an equity share in a young start-up counts towards your net worth, but that money likely won't do you any good until the company is sold, if they even make it that far! A diversified portfolio will make sure all your needs are covered.

That said, while you want to have multiple chickens laying eggs, you *don't* want to buy the whole farm, especially when you're just starting out. If you spread your money too thin across too many different assets, you probably won't be investing enough in each option to truly take advantage of the compounding that allows your money to grow. Apple stock might be profitable (sometimes), but if you only buy $100 of it, you won't be getting very far. You need to make sure you're investing enough in each option to make it worth its while, and that involves doing the math to figure out how your monthly amount will accumulate over time. How much is that $100/month investment going to be worth in five years? Ten? Twenty? Does that amount serve your purposes and meet your goals for this particular asset driver?

As your net worth increases and you have more income to invest, you'll be able to diversify your portfolio and invest in more options. You'll even be able to take more speculative risks and try new things just because you want to. As you move into the Stability stage and beyond, consider this as my recommended blend for asset distribution:

- 5-10% should go in an easily accessible liquid savings account.
- 20-30% should go in stable public securities, like an IRA or 401k.
- 60-75% should go into **one to three** primary asset drivers (not including public securities), which we'll discover in this chapter.

Again, of course, this is not a hard-and-fast rule. If, after exploring the other asset drivers in this chapter, you decide that investing more into public securities is the best option for your family, that's okay too. It may take you more time to meet your goals, but for some people, it might truly be the best option. But don't jump the gun before you've finished touring our financial "career fair." Make the effort to research some of the other options available to you and see if you can find a more effective, more profitable driver that works for your family.

By the same token, while I encourage you to research as many asset drivers as possible, for people in the Foundation stage of wealth creation, I whole-heartedly recommend that you only start with **one** primary asset driver (besides public securities). This is not only so that you don't spread your money too thin but also so that you have sufficient time and resources to become truly proficient in your chosen strategy.

So don't get overwhelmed as we go through this chapter. For now, let's focus on finding that *one* asset strategy that appeals to you, so you can get your journey started.

What About Retirement Plans?

People often ask me at this stage if their corporate retirement plan can be their primary asset driver. While retirement plans are a critical component of any healthy portfolio, I caution against making them your primary strategy. This is because the growth on most retirement plans is very slow, and your ability to increase your net worth to one million dollars will be dependent almost entirely on how much extra money you (and your employer) can put in each month (vA) and how long you're willing to wait (vD). While there are plenty of people who have done this successfully, my job is to encourage you to find the most *efficient* way to grow your money, and that involves exploring other asset options that yield higher returns.

This is also why we're going to emphasize the difference between passive and active strategies as we go through our various options. The goal of assets is to make our invested capital (our money) work for us—that is, to have our money make more money. This is called passive income, and it allows our wealth to increase without us needing to put in as many active work hours. There's nothing wrong with strategies that require your active involvement, but our long-term goal is to retire with less active work, so we need to prioritize developing passive income.

We also don't want to limit ourselves to our own physical ability. If our wealth-building plan is tied up entirely in active strategies that require our work hours, our ability to earn will always be limited by how much active effort we can put in. Since we all only have 24 hours in a day, this puts a definite cap on our earning potential. The more we can mobilize our wealth to passively grow on its own, the more our net worth can grow beyond our hourly limitations.

While retirement plans have a passive element to them, as they earn compound interest, the primary value of the account comes from how much you are able to put into it and how long you let it mature. For this reason, if you focus entirely on how much money you can put into your corporate plan, you are making your strategy entirely dependent on how many hours you can put in at work. Again, there are no wrong "solutions" to the wealth creation formula, but my job as a teacher is to encourage you to find the most *efficient* option, and corporate retirement plans are rarely your best bet.

So What's the Point?

With all the nuance involved in acquiring assets, it's easy to see how some people get lost and give up. If you're feeling overwhelmed and confused by all the options, take a step back and remind yourself why you're acquiring assets.

You are acquiring assets to build your net worth. An asset builds net worth because of its inherent value (i.e., the market value of a piece of real estate) and/or because it generates income (i.e., interest, or rent payments from tenants on a piece of real estate).

That's it. That is the sole purpose of acquiring assets. We're not getting into stocks for the sake of stocks; we're getting into stocks because they add to our net worth and propel us towards our goal. An asset's value boils down to the simple question: *How will this add to my net worth?* As you're evaluating various asset strategies, remember to pause and ask yourself:

1. *Does this asset have a value that will add to my net worth?*

2. *Will this asset generate income that will add to my net worth?*

The honest answers to those questions will tell you whether or not an asset is a responsible choice for you.

5 Common Asset Strategies

Now that we know why we acquire assets and how to effectively evaluate a potential strategy, it's time to take a tour of some of the diverse options available to us.

One thing to remember is that we are looking for assets that will appreciate in value and build our net worth over the next 10-20 years. This means we will not be discussing short-term options like day-trading stocks or flipping real estate. Most of those are income drivers rather than asset drivers, and while they are profitable options for some, they are not long-term investments and often require specialized knowledge or significant time investment. A busy father with five kids, a wife, and a full-time engineering job probably doesn't have the time to effectively develop a real-estate flipping business, but he can invest in rental properties that he holds onto for 20 years and earns passive rental income from. So that's where we'll keep our focus for the purpose of this chapter.

It's worth noting that many active strategies can be handled passively by hiring a manager to handle the day-to-day options. For example, you can either buy a rental property and handle all the administration yourself, or you can hire a property manager to do it for you. Which option is best for you depends on your competencies, available time, and any difference in profit outsourcing might cause. We're not going to spend extensive time in this chapter discussing the nuances of outsourcing and hiring managers. Just know that many asset strategies are convertible in this way.

Here are the five most common investment strategies I recommend to my students.

Public Securities

As I mentioned, I personally recommend that about 20-30% of your investable income be put into a stable public security, but I caution against making it your primary asset strategy because it can severely limit your earning power. Nevertheless, it's a viable part of most of the successful portfolios I've seen, so it's important to learn how stocks work and to be comfortable identifying plans that show proven returns. When you're researching public securities, remember that they come in many forms and go by many names, and each has their own set of risks and benefits:

- Individual public stocks (equity in a company)
- Individual private stocks (equity in a company)
- Mutual funds and ETFs (equity in many companies)
- Public bonds or U.S. treasuries (credit given to a company or government)
- Commodities (such as soybeans, oil, and coal)

For most investors, and especially people who are still in the Worry, Foundation, or Stability stages of wealth creation, I strongly recommend keeping your focus on public stocks and mutual funds. The other forms of investment come with more risks and require more knowledge, so if they interest you, I encourage you to research them more before investing.

The great thing about public securities is that they don't have to be complicated. There are many tools available now that make investing very easy and reliable. Whether it's a robo-advisor, a target date retirement fund, or industry-wide ETF, they all diversify your investments for you, making them sensible, generally safe long-term investments. Money Club has a course called Stocks & Investing 101, which simplifies investing and retirement accounts beautifully.

As a side note, if you're already contributing to an employer-backed retirement plan, now is a good time to review your benefits and make sure you fully understand the terms.

- Are you maximizing any employer matching programs?
- Are there conditions on when you can withdraw from the account?

Make sure you fully understand what you are getting into before you divert more of your paycheck into the program. You don't want to invest in a program that requires you to be with the company for 5 years before you own the account if you're planning on changing jobs before then. You'll also want to compare the potential returns of the corporate retirement plan to other public security investments you could seek out independently. Could you be earning more with your money somewhere else?

Real Estate

Real estate is one of the most well-known asset strategies outside of stock investing, and it's also a strategy that many people over-complicate. Developing real estate can be a living, so if you get your feet wet and discover that you love it, I encourage you to seek out additional education on the subject. For now, however, we are focusing on a very straightforward income-based model of leveraging real estate.

The model works like this:

- You purchase a rentable property, generally with 0-30% down and the rest borrowed.
- You rent the property out. (You can either manage the renting process yourself or hire a property manager.)
- The rent from the tenant pays the mortgage on the property.
- The rent payments gradually accumulate to make the property debt-free.
- The property is now a fully paid off asset (its debt-free market value is added to your net worth) and a source of income from the continuing rent payments.

At this point you'd have options. You could keep it as a continuing source of income, or you could sell or refinance it and use the money for something else, like another investment or your child's education fund.

That's all there is to it. Many people get lost in real estate because they either get neck-deep in a development project they can't handle (like buying homes to fix and flip) or because they think of the property as an income driver. To be successful in real estate, you have to think of it this way: The property is making you very little money until it is debt-free. Unless you are very disciplined to reinvest the cash flow, your best strategy is just to pay down the asset (the mortgage on the property). Once it's paid off, you can consider the property as a source of income and direct the cash flow accordingly.

If you keep this simple process in mind, anyone can handle real estate. Real estate is an ideal avenue for many, because it is entirely scalable. Even a busy family can usually manage one or two simple rental properties, and as you become more experienced in handling real estate, you can easily leverage your existing properties to buy more. Real estate also appreciates in value over time; because you are not trying to fix and flip, you can simply hold on to the property and weather any dips in the market. For these reasons and many more, I strongly recommend you research real estate and see if it is a viable option for you and your family.

Remember that real estate comes in many forms, each of which has different costs and risks associated with it:

- Single-family homes
- Mobile homes
- Industrial property
- Commercial/retail
- Multi-family homes/apartment buildings
- Self-storage
- Land
- RV/boat storage

- Rooms

The average family using real estate as an investment will likely focus on single-family homes and small multi-family units (such as townhomes, duplexes, and quadplexes), and I absolutely recommend that you start there. But if you find that you enjoy managing real estate, don't ignore the potential in larger units or commercial property.

Here are some questions to consider when evaluating if real estate is a good asset strategy for you:

1. How much actual cash can you contribute to purchase and manage the asset?
2. What are your property management skills? What time do you have available to manage the property?
3. Are you able to weather the ups and downs of the market until the property is paid off?
4. Are you willing and able to give it 15-20 years before the property is fully paid off?

Franchise Business

Investing in a business, whether buying into an existing one or building it from scratch, is a powerful double-edged asset strategy because it often drives both vA and vB at once. The business's regular profits can drive your income, while the business itself becomes a valuable asset that can later be sold for cash.

Naturally, however, getting into business is a multifaceted endeavor that generally requires active involvement. While it is possible to invest passively in businesses or outsource the daily management to others, most successful business investors are those who are personally and actively involved in the operations of the business on some level. That commitment isn't for everyone, but if you've ever thought about becoming self-employed, or you have a service, product, or interest that could be built into a business, you should strongly consider researching this option.

Of the various types of businesses, a franchise is appealing for many because the business model, brand, and product or service have already been proven. Much of the infrastructure is already there, including brand awareness and sales systems. This often makes the investment less risky than building an unproven startup from square one.

However, purchasing a franchise usually requires a larger sum of money upfront. If you cannot afford the entire amount upfront, you will have to finance the balance. While my son was in college, he worked at a franchise that was owned by a 28-year-old who did just that. He purchased the franchise for $25,000 down, financing the remaining $125,000 through the corporate office itself. Seven years after his initial investment, the franchise produced over $120,000 a year in net income and was valued at $1.2 million. It's worth noting that the young franchise owner had hardly any investable income during those first seven years, and yet he grew both his income and his asset value to extraordinary levels in less than a decade.

Like most businesses, a franchise generally requires that you be actively involved in the success of the business until you can promote a manager you trust. Some other questions to consider if you're looking into franchise investment:

1. How much actual cash can you contribute to acquisition and management?
2. What skills does the investor/franchise owner need?
3. What will the time commitment of owning this small business be?

Non-Franchise Small Business Startup

Instead of buying into an existing franchise, another viable asset strategy is to start and run your own business. This is the epitome of the American Dream, and millions of people have found success in becoming small business owners.

Of course, a "small business" can mean almost anything from walking dogs and selling art on Etsy to publishing books or starting a plumbing business. The difficulty many people run into when considering a small business proposition is that they confuse income drivers with asset drivers.

As we've mentioned, a business can either bring you income or be a valuable asset that could be sold for cash. Many times, it's both. And while both are valid reasons to develop a business, you need to have a very clear idea of what role this business is playing in your wealth creation plan, especially in the long run over 10-20 years. If you develop a business primarily for the cash flow, you will then probably need another asset to pour your personal investable income into. Similarly, if you develop a business for its asset value, you need to have a clear idea of what the business is worth and how you can grow its value.

Consider again the example of my freelance editor. Her freelance editing business is primarily an income driver. Although she could theoretically build the brand into an asset that could be sold, this is unlikely since the value of her company is based primarily on her and her work. If, however, she diversified and built a publishing company, that publishing brand, as well as the creative properties under its label, could become valuable assets that could be sold for cash. Neither of these are wrong options, but she needs to have a clear idea of her purpose for her company as she's making her long-term plan for wealth.

Another angle to consider is that investing in a small business doesn't always mean starting a mom-and-pop store that is entirely dependent on you and your skills. A small business can also include being an independent salesperson or being a partner in a company. All of these require unique skills and dispositions, so I encourage you to carefully consider your core competencies when evaluating any potential business option.

Some other factors to consider:

1. How much actual cash will you need to start the business?
2. Are you willing to invest in educating yourself on how to start and run the business?
3. Have you determined what type of business is best for you?
4. Have you analyzed and thoroughly researched your potential business?
5. With regards to this specific business, are your skills more closely aligned with being a technician (actively producing the product or service) or a manager (managing others who produce the product or service)?
6. What role will you need to play in this business to make it successful? What role will you enjoy?

7. Is there evidence that time and capital will produce a valuable asset?
8. What will the value of the business be in 5, 10, or 20 years?
9. What is the risk of losing the up-front investment compared to the reward of the asset value?

Mortgages and Mortgage Lending

One of the least-known investment strategies available to individuals is lending money. Lending money is one of the oldest businesses in the world. There are an endless number of ways to profit off of lending money, but many of them fall under income drivers. For the purposes of building long-term assets, I want to focus only on secured lending.

A secured loan is simply a loan that is backed by the value of a tangible asset. For example, a home equity line of credit uses your home as collateral, or "protection," against a cash loan. In fact, loans secured by real estate are the most common type of secured lending. This practice is commonly called **mortgage lending** or **mortgage investing**.

The main benefits of providing real estate-secured loans are that, when handled wisely, your capital is secured by a hard asset (the property) and you have a more predictable rate of return. Additionally, you can usually predict and prepare for what would happen in a worst-case scenario if a borrower were to default on a loan.

This is why I often speak of mortgage lending as a fixed income alternative that yields much higher rates. A fixed income alternative is an investment that is very low risk and provides you with a steady, albeit small, stream of regular income. Examples include treasury or corporate bonds, CDs, money market accounts, etc. These are great investments to protect a portion of your assets, but they typically only yield about a 1-5% return, which is lower than the stock market and often can't keep up with inflation (which averages about 2-3%). However, as I described above, mortgage lending is particularly appealing to investors because the loan is secured by a tangible asset and can provide up to an 8-12% return of fixed steady income from the interest payments.

Like all other types of lending, mortgage lending and investing can be both an income driver and an asset driver. A person that invests his/her own money in real estate mortgages solves vB. A person that makes an active living writing mortgages using other people's money is solving vA, unless they are building a business brand that has asset value. One could also build a mortgage lending business and use part or all of their own money for lending, which would solve both variables.

There are nuances here that require more depth than this book allows. If you are looking for a new or additional income driver, I highly encourage you to consider building a small business as a mortgage broker, mortgage banker, or private lender. You can focus full- or part-time on either residential or commercial loans, or both. Separately, you can simply invest with a private equity fund, like the one I manage, that invests your money for you.

Like investing in real estate, mortgages are high-ticket items with great potential returns, and if I have the option to coach someone towards a big-ticket item rather than dealing in pennies and dimes, I will. I also like the mortgage business because, for most people, it only requires knowledge and effort to make significant money as a vA solution; a formal degree is not required, and there is little start-up infrastructure needed. In this section, however, we are focused on being the lender, or investing with lenders, and utilizing mortgages as an investment strategy.

Like all the other strategies we discussed in this chapter, you'll want to educate yourself on the breadth and depth of the strategy you choose. You want to increase your specialized knowledge and eventually become an expert in your chosen area. Mortgage lending is no exception. If this appeals to you, I highly recommend you start researching your options today.

After Step 3

Unlike the other two steps in our wealth creation plan, Step 3 doesn't have a clearly defined "end." The goal of Step 3 is to get you settled into a long-term asset strategy that you can use to grow your wealth over the next 10-20 years. Once you've found the strategy that works for you, your primary focus should shift to maximizing that strategy and growing your assets. You should now be measuring your progress primarily with financial milestones as you move from the Worry stage through the Foundation stage and into the Stability stage and beyond.

However, you should always keep an open mind about asset strategies and continually be on the lookout for new and better opportunities. Your financial portfolio should change with you, especially as your net worth grows and you have more investable income at your disposal. In a way, we never really leave Step 3, because we are always searching for the most efficient way to make our money work for us.

Remember that, until you transition into the Stability stage, you should still be spending about ten hours earning and two hours learning each day. This isn't a science, of course, and depending on how quickly you develop passive streams of income, the focus of your earning time will shift dramatically as your financial outlook matures. But I want to caution you against taking your foot off the gas too early. I have seen many people stifle their long-term growth because they grew complacent or distracted. It's very easy to just throw some money in an IRA and think you've done enough. It's even easier to lose your initial momentum after you've been working on the same plan for one, two, five, or ten years.

The fervor that you began this journey with will not last unless you make a concentrated effort to keep yourself motivated and driven. Make it a priority to keep your goals and financial vision fresh and in the forefront of your mind. Keep a list of your motivations—like the one we worked on back in Chapter 5—where you can see it. Refer to it and update it often. Enlist the accountability of positive financial influencers in your life. Constantly come up with new challenges, milestones, and intermediate goals for yourself. Design a structure of rewards along the way to congratulate yourself for hard-earned progress. Reassess your financial situation annually to make sure you're still on track with your goals—and to fully appreciate how far you've come.

As you move into Step 3 and beyond, both your earning and learning time should be highly focused. Your earning time should be spent exclusively on developing your primary income driver (which you determined in Step 2) and building your most effective asset strategies. If you picked up temporary work to boost your investable income, you should be diligent about building passive income from your asset streams so that you can eventually drop the side job and pour your time into something more profitable.

Your learning time will be devoted primarily to building your expertise in your chosen asset strategy, as well as continuing to raise your value in your primary career field, if applicable. However, as you grow more comfortable in your asset strategies, you should also begin investing in your personal development. Ask yourself, *"When I get to the Growth and Freedom stages, who do I want to be? What do I want to do?"* When we worked on our financial motivations in Chapter 5, we wrote down what we wanted to do with financial freedom when we had it. Look back at that list: Who is that person? Are there any skills they are going to need? What character traits and life values are important to them? How can you begin training yourself to become that person?

One final note on time: During Step 3, it is critical that you constantly evaluate the opportunity cost of the time you spend on various activities. During Steps 1 and 2, when our primary focus was to lower our expenses and eliminate debt, there were things that we did ourselves because they were cheaper. Now that you're developing your long-term income and asset drivers, you may find that you're actually losing money on those activities because they are detracting from time you could be spending earning.

Here's an example. My wife used to ask me why I didn't just mow our lawn myself and save the money we spent on yard service. I did the math to show her that me doing the lawn myself would actually cause us to *lose* money, and a great deal of it. In the time I would have spent doing the lawn each month, I could typically make about $1,000. Therefore, it was much more profitable for me to pay someone else $100 to do the lawn so I could continue to focus on growing our net worth.

The situation is different for everyone, and early on you will probably need to do a lot of things yourself to save money. But as you grow financially, keep a close eye on how you're using your time and critically evaluate the actual cost of those hours. Just like everything else, your schedule is going to change with you, so be flexible and ready to adapt.

Even though we've come to the end of our three-step plan, there are still two more variables to discover in the wealth creation formula. It's time to unlock the silent "secret ingredients" that will cause your money to multiply exponentially: Leverage and Time.

CASE STUDY #5

Steve K., Atlanta, GA

Unlike many of my other interviewees, Steve obtained an undergraduate degree in engineering and an MBA from an Ivy League school. He was a bright student, securing mostly As in college. At the time of his interview, Steve was 55 years old. I couldn't be more thrilled to sit down and exchange words with him. The reason? Steve's net worth is a *whopping 35 million dollars.*

He currently works as a partner in a private business he invested in a few years ago. His average annual income over the past three years was $400k, of which $280k was passive income. Just like other self-made millionaires, he did not inherit any of his wealth.

His first job was as a general electrician designing satellites. His second job was as a consultant at Deloitte. By the time Steve was 27 years old, he was already making $110k per year, and by age 37, he had increased his net worth to $500k.

Looking for this third job, Steve ended up going to a dotcom startup and received stock options which became valuable over time. The price of his stocks went from $6/share to $200/share. When the company was sold, it was a burst of gleaming sunshine for Steve: He made 15 million dollars in one swoop. He decided to retire at age 39.

Despite this stroke of luck, Steve's road to success has been filled with plenty of spikes and sharp curves. In particular, Steve committed a fatal error by handing much of his net worth to a money manager who stole almost all of it and left Steve with nothing. He had no choice but to start over. To pour salt on an open wound, Steve was also diagnosed with cancer around the same time.

Nevertheless, Steve persevered and survived cancer like a hero. When he was back in action, he invested $200k into a methadone clinic business, for which he acted as a consultant. This was his fourth job. After four years, the business was partially sold, and Steve received 10 million dollars for his 50% ownership. Today, Steve still has ownership in the same methadone clinic business and receives a salary, although he is not very actively involved.

For the last 15-18 years, Steve has been investing in venture capital. He, too, felt like he could be more successful on his own, which is why he became his own boss and devoted most of his efforts into generating his own income, rather than relying on a salary.

As far as the financial influence he received growing up, Steve lost his mother when young, and his dad only had a high-school education. Nevertheless, Steve had peers who encouraged him towards his goals and teachers who recognized his intelligence. Even though he went to private school, Steve confided in me that one turning point in his life was when he realized that his wealthy classmates were no smarter than he was. If they could obtain wealth, surely he could, too!

Steve's path to generating investable income was tumultuous, to say the least. He did not have any investable income in his early 20s. However, during his late 20s he managed a salary of $40k per year. That gradually increased to $110k, and then his income leaped drastically when he had his 15-million-dollar windfall. After that, most of his investable income has been derived from passive investments.

Steve built his vA solution much in the same way Henry did: by going to college and obtaining a degree while working really hard to land multiple high-income jobs. Later he cleared his vB solution by investing in the following:

1. Public stocks and bonds (>10%)
2. Private and public businesses (80%)
3. Real estate (>5%)

When I asked him to provide his advice on wealth creation, he replied: "I was able to build my fortune because of my aggressive attitude and ability to take risks. There are three things that I lived by to create my wealth. They are:

1. Live conservatively so that you can take risks.
2. Take calculated risks and look for opportunities in everyday life.
3. Learn to live with less structure and more ambiguity."

In summary, Steve utilized his education and jobs to prepare him to join a startup that propelled him to have a liquidity event. His ability to effectively identify and invest in companies is evidenced by the two substantial liquidity events he had. In this case study, one could argue that Steve excelled in school and in identifying where to invest for maximum appreciation of his time and capital. My personal take? Steve is a unique and gifted individual with a knack for backing the right vehicle.

You start becoming wealthy the minute you comprehend the true power that leverage and compounding hold.

EIGHT

The Power of Leverage

The variables we will discuss in the following two chapters are your most powerful tools for wealth creation. Even though most of our conscious energy is consumed with developing income and assets, the other two components—time and leverage—are the unseen magic that make your money multiply. Without the effects of variables vC and vD, both income and assets would be static and immobile, and we may as well just stockpile rolls of cash in our mattresses. Leverage and time are what make money multiply, and without them it would be impossible to develop passive income.

Another reason leverage and time are so powerful is that they are frequently misunderstood and infrequently taught. Very few schools truly teach people how to maximize these variables, and most of our financial influencers do not know how to manage these valuable resources. The mastery of leverage and time is the defining characteristic that separates the wealthy from wage earners. Let's tackle leverage first.

Leverage

The world and all its wealth operate on leverage. I believe leverage is one of the most powerful concepts in business and finance, perhaps second only to the effective use of time, and it has profound effects on our everyday life, too.

What is leverage? In a basic sense, leverage is simply the act of using something (or someone) to a greater advantage. In financial terms, leverage is using borrowed money to increase the potential return of a business or investment. For most of our everyday applications, leverage means to use borrowed money for investment with the expectation that earnings will outweigh the total amount (principal + interest) owed on the debt. In the wealth creation formula, you can think of leverage as the ability to acquire more asset value (vB) with less investable income (vA) and/or time (vD).

Like time, leverage is not a freestanding asset that you can earn or purchase. **Leverage is a variable that operates within your income and asset drivers whether you realize it or not.** Chances are, if you're not using leverage to your advantage, someone else is leveraging you or your money to their advantage. Succeeding financially involves understanding the concept of leverage and applying it to your situation so that your money works for you instead of against you.

Leverage might sound like a daunting concept, but believe it or not, you probably use leverage every day without even realizing it. If you have a mortgage on your home, you're using leverage. You invested a comparatively small amount of your own money (your down payment) and borrowed the rest from the bank. By using the bank's money to buy a house, you used leverage to acquire an asset (the house) that was worth far more than the cash you invested (your down payment). In other words, you bought a home valued at $120,000 with only $24,000 down, maybe less. That's leverage.

Another everyday form of leverage is wage-earning. When an auto shop pays a mechanic $30/hour to repair cars but then charges the customer $60/hour in labor, the company has leveraged a person's time and energy (the mechanic) to make a profit.

Buying stocks on margin, purchasing a business using an SBA loan, and acquiring a rental property using a mortgage are all examples of utilizing leverage. Specifically, these are all examples of leveraging money. Leveraging money is, of course, the most common kind of leverage; we spent a great deal of time in Steps 2 and 3 learning how to leverage our money (investable income) to create more money (passive income, appreciating assets, etc.). But money isn't the only resource we can leverage. We can leverage people, knowledge, and assets as well.

This is why I balk when people complain that they "need money to make money" or that their only path to wealth requires more starting capital. If you believe the only path to wealth is to generate more gross income or purchase more raw assets, then you haven't fully unlocked the power of leverage in your financial life.

As soon as you learn to activate the leveraging power of *all* your resources, not just your money, you will liberate yourself to truly multiply your net worth.

Leveraging People

There are many ways to leverage people. All businesses leverage people when they use labor to produce a more-valuable good or service. Delegation of tasks, both at work and outside of it, is leverage. Even households leverage people. When I tell my son to take out the trash, I'm leveraging him. When I hire someone for $100/month to mow my lawn so I can make $1,000 with those redeemed hours, I'm leveraging my lawn care service.

For those of you who are looking at building businesses, whether as an income or asset driver, leveraging people may be your greatest area of opportunity for increasing profit. Consider the example of a housecleaning business. If one person cleans houses by themselves and charges $30/hour, they can make $1,200/week. But if they hire 3 additional people and pay them $15/hour, collectively the company can now clean $4,800 worth of houses a week, of which the owner is making $2,400. Not only did the owner grow their business (which is an asset) far beyond what they could by relying on their own labor, but they also doubled their income while working the same number of hours per week. This is just one example of how someone can use leverage to increase their income.

Another great example of leveraging people is by investing in rental properties. You can purchase a property by leveraging the bank's money, as described above, and then rent the property out for someone to live or work in. You are providing them a critical service and they are contributing their money to pay down your loan for you, ultimately giving you more equity in your asset without any additional financial investment of your own (besides repairs and upgrades).

As with many things in life, people are your most powerful source of value. They have money, time, energy, knowledge, etc. But this is not to say that your interactions with people need to be transactional. It's important to understand the value you can get from a relationship, but just as important is to understand the value that you can genuinely provide to a relationship. That is the bedrock of a sustainable and reliable investment. By investing your own resources (time, energy, knowledge, money, etc.) into your relationships, you are building trust and social equity. Invest in people for the right reasons and the value you get from them will be abundant and long-lasting. This is also one of many reasons why I advise people to invest heavily in learning about psychology and personal development; it can earn you dividends in your relationships.

Leveraging Knowledge

Knowledge is a two-edged sword when it comes to leverage. First, you need knowledge to understand leverage so you can make it work for you. But once you understand leverage, you can then turn around and leverage your knowledge—your financial literacy, your college degree, your unique competencies and talents—to make money.

Most parents and educators understand this primal concept, which is why many of them believe so strongly in the necessity of college. They recognize that there's a correlation between having a college degree and securing a higher-paying job; in other words, degree-earners leverage their specialized knowledge to demand higher wages. Of course, we understand that a college education is not required for all paths to wealth, but this is a good demonstration of how knowledge can be leveraged.

There are two types of knowledge we can leverage: foundational knowledge and specialized knowledge. Foundational knowledge is basic competency skills like reading, writing, math, science, and physical education, as well as interpersonal skills like social interaction and communication. Specialized knowledge is that which qualifies you to perform within a specific field. If you know how to service cars, that's specialized knowledge. Within fields there is usually a further hierarchy of specialized knowledge. The more of an expert someone is in their field, the more they can leverage their specialized knowledge.

The most common way we leverage knowledge is by leveraging information and basic skills to gain specialized knowledge. You can use books, YouTube, online courses, and podcasts to train yourself in any new skill. In other words, you leverage basic information (i.e., the fact that you can request books from the library) to gain specialized knowledge (the content of the books). When I was starting out, I leveraged the information that one of my neighbors was a real estate agent to borrow books on the subject and ultimately gain the connection that changed my life. These are the everyday, transactional ways we leverage knowledge.

Remember that something can only be leveraged if it has inherent value. Chatting about stocks with your friend who doesn't have any financial experience is not a leveraging conversation.

If you're looking to leverage knowledge to increase your earning potential, here are some of the questions you should ask yourself:

- Do you consider yourself an expert in your profession?
- Do others consider you an expert?
- Do you earn the same as the other experts in your profession?
- In what areas do you need to improve to become an expert?
- If you become an expert, will the industry pay you considerably more for this expertise?
- Is there a measurable value in the marketplace for you if you become an expert?
- Should you become an expert in your current profession or become an expert in another profession to earn the level of income you require?

Knowledge truly is power! Remember, the book you don't read can't help you, so never be ashamed to admit when you lack the foundational or specialized knowledge you need to succeed to your fullest potential. You are never too old to learn. As someone who got terrible grades in high school and never went to college, I am living proof that knowledge is available to everyone regardless of their disposition or the setbacks they've experienced. One of the few major regrets I have about my life is that I did not truly appreciate the value of knowledge until my early 20s. Begin today to respect the importance of knowledge in your life. It is truly more valuable than money.

Leveraging Assets

Like cash, assets can be leveraged to acquire more assets or money. In fact, that is the primary reason we purchase assets; we invest a certain amount of money into them on the expectation that they will one day be worth more. However, as you gain experience and knowledge in your field, you'll find there are often more advanced ways to leverage your assets to acquire more assets.

For example, if I own $20,000 worth of Apple stock and want to purchase $10,000 more, I can borrow against my $20,000 by pledging the entire $30,000 as security for the loan. This is called borrowing on margin.

Another common method of leverage is to secure mortgages with existing property as collateral to buy more property—that is, taking out a loan that is secured by the property you already own, also known as refinancing. Sometimes you can even use both properties as collateral—the one you currently own and the one you are intending to buy—to secure a loan that far exceeds the value of the cash you put down upfront.

Of course, all debt comes with risks, and a smart investor knows how to balance those risks. This includes having the clear ability to weather dips in the market and manage the debt until it is paid in full. Many people simply do not have this knowledge or ability, which is why you'll see many financial advisors like Dave Ramsey cautioning people against using debt to acquire assets. Like all investment strategies, if you're going to do it effectively, you'll need to do your research and gain the specialized knowledge required.

Even more importantly, to get to more advanced levels of risk- and reward-taking with leveraging assets, you need to build a strong foundation of healthy money behaviors and mindsets. If you have not yet curbed your bad spending habit or managed your daily budget, you will not be able to handle the responsibility of leverage, and taking on debt will only propel you in the wrong direction faster. Also remember that all of your liabilities count against your total net worth. If you acquire assets through debt without having a defined, attainable plan for paying off that debt, your net worth will not increase overall.

Leveraging Money

Even though it is far from the only means of leverage, money is still a highly effective leverage tool. We've already explored many examples of how to leverage money. All of the asset strategies we discussed in the previous chapter rely heavily on leveraging money to acquire an appreciable asset. The 28-year-old franchisee my son worked for leveraged the corporate office to purchase a business that was eventually valued at $1.2 million, all for a mere down payment of $25,000.

Personally, my favorite example of leveraging money is mortgage lending. As you'll see in the example below, by borrowing money at a low interest rate and lending at a higher interest rate you can nearly double your rate of return from the same investment.

Imagine that you worked hard and saved $33,000. After researching the technical and legal considerations of lending money, you could engage in either of these lending scenarios. (Numbers have been rounded for the purpose of this example.)

Scenario 1: A friend of yours wants to borrow $33,000 for 24 months. He already owns a rental property, and you agree to lend him the money secured by that property. The borrower (your friend the real estate owner) agrees to pay you 9.5% annually for the money. You earn $3,000 per year in income.

Scenario 2: A friend of yours wants to borrow $100,000 for 24 months. He already owns a rental property, and you agree to lend him the money secured by that property. You only have $33,000, but you access a line of credit through your bank. As long as you pledge the $100,000 mortgage as collateral, the bank will agree to advance you $67,000.

You loaned $100,000 to your real estate investor friend at an interest rate of 9.5%. Your bank loaned you $67,000 at an interest rate of 5.5%. The breakdown below demonstrates the annual rate of return on your own $33,000:

- The total amount loaned to your friend: $100,000
- The amount of your own money that you used: $33,000
- The amount that the bank loaned to you: $67,000
- The interest your friend pays each year at 9.5% on $100,000: $9,500
- The annual payment you make to the bank at 5.5% on $67,000: $3,600
- The difference between what your friend is paying you and what you must pay to the bank: **$5,900**

When you calculate the annual rate of return on your investment in each of these scenarios you get:

- **Scenario 1**: $3,000 or 9.5% on your investment of $33,000
- **Scenario 2**: $5,900 or 17.5% on your investment of $33,000

Both scenarios utilized the same amount of your own money, but one brought nearly double the return. The key difference, of course, was the effective use of leverage.

This example just scrapes the surface of the potential earnings in secured mortgage lending. You can employ this same strategy to yield even higher rates of return. If you want to learn more about lending money, please see my other book titled *Be the Bank*, which will teach you how to increase wealth through private mortgage lending.

To review, in each example of leverage discussed in this chapter, we leveraged a comparatively small amount of resources—whether that be money, labor, knowledge, or assets—to acquire resources of far greater value. Leverage, paired with the principles of time and compounding, is the variable that will unlock your earning potential and allow you to multiply your wealth far above your wages. This is how wealth is created—not by stockpiling income, but by positioning your money and assets so that they can make money for themselves. Let's unlock the final ingredient that will make that magic happen for us: Time.

CASE STUDY #6

Dan C., Maryland

Dan earned two master's degrees from John Hopkins—the first in finance and the second an MBA. He was a shining bud in college with grades in the As and Bs. He was 51 when we sat belly to belly for the interview, and his net worth was an astounding 11 million dollars.

He did not inherit any of his wealth from family members, and the main reason he went to college was because he received a free year at a community college. During his first few years of college, he worked full time as an electrician. He later dropped out of community college and went to a local state school. He always believed that the employment world was fierce and that he needed a 4-year degree to compete. That's why he paid for his own college, partially through

PELL grants. It took him 6 years to get through undergrad, all while working the entire time.

His first job was working as an electrician while he was a student at Tech High School and during college. His second job started two months after college as an insurance underwriter, where he earned $20k per year. His third job was with an insurance third party administrator. There, his boss—the first high-earner Dan was in close contact with—became an important financial influencer. His approach was to teach Dan how to win.

Dan earned $50k working at that company. After a while, Dan recognized that he needed to be in sales if he wanted to make a lot of money. Although he was a technical guy by nature, he believed he could set up the processes and do very well in sales. He spent 22 years in sales. His yearly salary was $125k, which he increased to $750K by his late 30s—pretty cool, isn't it? His current job is as a regional sales manager at a large insurance company. Even after making a lot of money, Dan never sought self-employment.

Growing up, Dan lost his father when he was 2 years old, and his mother bootstrapped raising him. He did not have any positive financial influence except one friend, who became a profitable landlord after college, and his second employer, who taught Dan how to go for the gold. For the most part he was self-taught.

It was clear that Dan was making a lot of money. Here is a table to illustrate Dan's growing investable income with age:

Dan's Age	Annual Investable Income
20-30	$12k (401k contributions)
30-40	$50k-$150k
40-50	$250k-$500k

Dan also solved his asset strategy by investing in the following:

1. Public stocks and bonds: He maximized corporate benefits with employer matching, then later put 30-35% of his assets into passive investment funds.
2. Real estate: He bought income properties for 17 years, buying higher-valued properties as his passive income increased.
3. Private mortgages.

When I asked him what he thought were the key drivers on the path to wealth, he responded: "There are many things you need to do to become wealthy, all of which I put into practice in my own life. If I were to advise you on a few specific things, it would be the following:

1. Start with being competitive with yourself. Always try to get better without excuses. Grit and grind.
2. You must understand that it takes time and patience, but always think bigger.
3. Be prudent with your risk; stay in your financial category.
4. You must be passionate and committed.
5. Surround yourself with the right people.
6. If you don't have money, find people with money."

In summary, Dan had a great success story of first putting himself through college, then learning the insurance business, where he excelled in sales. This earned him a very high income, which he poured into various assets. He is the quintessential example of the wealth formula being executed on all four cylinders with great success.

Time is what we want most,
but what we use worst.
—William Penn

NINE

The Role of Time

We have talked extensively about how time is not only a variable but also a resource in and of itself. How you manage your time is probably the sole most important determinant of your success. All of the other variables are worthless to you if you do not properly invest your time into them, and effective use of time can offset even the greatest disadvantages elsewhere. Someone with low-income and limited financial knowledge who manages their time expertly will most likely go farther than someone with both assets and intelligence but who fails to structure their day wisely.

However, in addition to managing our daily ration of 24 hours (short-term use of time), we need to understand that time is a variable that operates continually, whether we are conscious of it or not. Time is constantly passing, altering our equation of wealth with every week, month, and year that ticks by. This is the long-term use of time, and it has an enormous impact on our ability to grow wealth far beyond our wage-earning potential. If we effectively use time long-term, we will leverage it to multiply our assets. If we poorly manage time long-term, however, it will work against us and ultimately depreciate our assets.

Let's use a child's savings of $100 as an extremely basic example. That child can either put their $100 in a retirement savings account, where it will earn a considerable amount of interest over time, or they can keep it in rolls of quarters under their bed. The cash in the retirement account will increase in value over time; the quarters under the bed will actually decrease in value as inflation weakens their buying power. The same principle affects both our income and our assets on a larger scale. Simply ignoring the passage of time will have devastating effects on our overall net worth, but effectively utilizing time will cause our assets to multiply, often with minimal active involvement from ourselves.

The variable of time affects our equation in a variety of ways. At a primal level, we need to be willing to invest time to properly develop all of our other variables. It takes time to learn about investing through mortgage lending, for example, and even more time to become an expert at it. It takes time to build a retirement account to a sufficient level. It takes time to grow a business to the point where it's valuable enough to be sold for cash. These are all elaborate ways of saying we need patience, consistency, and perseverance.

Time also affects the value of our assets, especially when we're looking 10-20 years into the future. Consider some of the following examples:

- The market value of a business often increases the longer it has been in operation.
- The market value of a business increases as revenue increases year over year.
- The value of real estate typically increases over time and as the mortgage is paid down.
- The value of savings accounts, public securities, and other investments typically increases over time as interest compounds.

That last factor is probably the most profound, but before we dive into the principle of compounding interest, let's explore the different ways time causes assets to increase in value.

Appreciation, Amortization, & Depreciation

The reason why time is the final variable we discuss in the wealth formula is that it is most powerful when we build it upon the other three. Once we develop a steady stream of investable income, we can use leverage to acquire and mature assets. As discussed, assets can become a powerful leverage tool in and of themselves, but even if we didn't touch them, time would still cause most of them to gradually increase in value.

Think back to the basic rental property model we discussed in Chapter 7. You acquire a real estate property by investing some of your own cash up front, leveraging a bank to finance the remainder with a mortgage. You then rent the property out, which leverages another person's time and money to gradually pay down the mortgage. Even without investing any more of your own money into the equity of the house, time will increase your net worth through this asset in three important ways:

1. Each month that passes, your property may increase in value as real estate values inflate. Like the stock market, this is never guaranteed, and there will be seasons where the market dips. But if you consider the long-term progress of the market, since 1953 there

has been a steady increase in real estate values[7]. This is called appreciation.
2. Each month that passes, your tenant is paying down another increment of your mortgage, thereby decreasing your debt and increasing your net worth. This is called amortization.
3. Each year that passes, you can write off a portion of the asset's value from your taxes. For example, on a $200k property, you can write off about $7,000 each year from your taxes over a 27-year period. This is called tax depreciation.

Remember, since the money earned from appreciation or amortization is not accessible to us unless we sell the property, it is not liquid. However, it is contributing to our net worth. Putting all of these factors together, we can surmise that we would collect a much larger lump sum by selling the property 15 years after purchase versus only 5 years after purchase, all while investing very little additional resources of our own. By simply letting leverage and time work their magic, we have drastically increased our earnings and net worth.

---

[7] http://www.econ.yale.edu/~shiller/data.htm

Compounding

Most people are familiar with the basic concept of compounding interest. Time is what makes interest valuable, because the longer the investment account is open, the more interest accrues. The earlier you are able to begin investing, and the longer you are able to let interest work, the greater your returns.

Many of the world's up-and-coming millionaires are not professional investors like Warren Buffet. They are not dealing in risky speculations or aggressively flipping real estate. They simply make a concerted effort to dedicate a high amount of investable income over an extended period of time. In other words, if all you did was pour your $1,600/month of investable income into some kind of income/interest-bearing account like a public security, and continued to do so for several decades, you would, without fail, become a millionaire. It really is that simple to build wealth if you let time do the work for you.

On the other hand, it is nearly impossible to gain back the monetary value of wasted time. Throwing large amounts of money at an investment later in life almost never yields the same return as a much smaller amount invested earlier. Time is truly more valuable than money, and it is extraordinarily difficult to become wealthy without it.

This is why they say the "rich get richer and the poor get poorer." The poor's assets are not working for them; their money is tied up in cash and household goods that depreciate in value rather than appreciate. But the rich's money, even when it is invested in something as simple as an IRA, is appreciating with the passage of time. Even if they do nothing, the rich will literally get richer.

Let's look at some specific examples of how this works. Compounding is the simple act of having interest or dividends added onto the principal balance, so that it can earn more interest. For example, if we invest $100 at a 10% rate of return, we'll earn $10 in the first year. If we withdraw that $10 and leave the $100 in the bank to earn another $10 next year, that's simple interest. Compound interest is when we leave that $10 in the bank so we can earn 10% on $110 and make $11 next year. Time will continue this process ad infinitum if we let it. This is why even the most basic investment strategies, like retirement plans and other public securities, function on compound interest. It is extraordinarily difficult to build wealth over the long-term without it. Consider:

- Invest $500 a month in a regular savings account and you'd end up with $240k in 40 years.

- Invest $500 a month in a retirement account earning 6% compound interest/dividend, and you'd get $933k in the same forty years!

It's no wonder Albert Einstein called compounding "the eighth wonder of the world." He went on to say that "He who understands it, earns it. He who doesn't, pays it." Truer words were never spoken! Credit cards, student loans, and personal loans all use compounding to calculate the interest you owe to your creditors. Use compounding interest in your favor, however, and you will watch your investments balloon over time.

Compounding interest is the epitome of passive income. With it, even the simplest investments, when allowed to mature for 15+ years, can net us hundreds of thousands or even millions. Without it, however, all of your income and asset drivers would be entirely dependent on your active involvement. Compound interest is the closest thing we get to free money. Accounts without compound interest, however, only grow if we put more money in.

While the time the account is allowed to accrue is the biggest factor that determines how much you can earn with compounding interest, several other numbers factor into the equation:

- The amount of the initial investment
- The amount and frequency of any subsequent investments
- The rate of return on the investment
- The frequency of applying the interest or dividend to the principal balance (quarterly, annually, etc.)
- If any withdrawals are made from the investment

Compounding is often discussed primarily in regards to public securities, but it is just as powerful a force in any kind of asset. The more employees a business hires, the faster it can grow its sales. The more rent you collect from existing properties, the faster you can acquire new properties. The more you reinvest your interest into a private equity fund, the faster your fund can grow. The core principle of compounding in all of these examples is that the earnings are reinvested. If you take your earnings to buy a second sports car, that sports car does nothing to increase your wealth. But the more you reinvest your earnings during each stage of your journey, the faster your rate of growth increases.

The influence of time and compounding on our ability to build wealth is why I encouraged you early on in Step 1 to begin investing in public securities. This simple action allowed you to start taking advantage of both time and compounding while you were addressing your immediate needs of budgeting, debt payoff, and education. Since the moment you made your first deposit into your account, time and compounding have been making you money without you having to do a single thing.

This is also why I implore my younger readers to immediately start dedicating as much of their income as they can to investments, especially while they have lower living expenses. The sooner you begin investing, the wealthier you will be when you retire, even if you do nothing else with your investable income. The effect of time and compounding is so profound that you can even stop investing midway through life, if you start young, and still end up with more money than someone who starts later.

Many people have broken down the mathematics on this, but my favorite explanation is from Alaina Tweddale on *Money Under 30*[8]. In her example, three fictional investors invest $12,000 a year for 10 years, starting at age 25, 35, and 45, respectively. They made no further investments after those ten years. When all three retired at 65, one was a millionaire. The other two were not. Can you guess which one retired with seven digits?

---

[8] https://www.moneyunder30.com/power-of-compound-interest

CASE STUDY #7

Bobby G., Washington, D.C.

Bobby was a good student, always getting As and Bs in college. After obtaining his master's degree, he worked as a partner in a private equity firm. At the time of his interview, he was 70 years old. His net worth was 15 million dollars and his average annual income over the past three years was $250k. His wife also made $225k per year—a pretty neat couple, aren't they?

Unlike the other millionaires I interviewed for this book, Bobby did inherit a small portion of his net worth from family members, but the majority of it he built himself.

Like the others, Bobby worked an eclectic assortment of jobs. His first job was as an auto mechanic; his second job was as a computer manager for a non-profit company; and his third job was at a business school, which led into consulting.

He then became self-employed as an independent consultant at age 35, which he continued to do for the next 28 years. Currently, he is retired and enjoying life. Interestingly, Bobby originally became self-employed not by choice but because he had lost his job. However, he seized the opportunity and maximized the potential.

Growing up, Bobby did not have strong financial influence until graduate school, except for his uncles and a few teachers. His first employer after graduating was also a fair influence.

To create his vA solution, Bobby went to college and obtained a degree, then worked extremely hard to achieve as many high-income jobs as possible. Here is a table to illustrate his investable income by age:

Bobby's Age	Annual Investable Income
20-30	None
30-40	$10k-$20k
40-50	$20k-$30k
50-60	$50k-$100k
60-70	$50k-$2.5mil

Bobby invested in multiple areas to solve his variable vB. Here is a breakdown of his investments:

- Public stocks and bonds (~10-15% of his net worth)

- Private businesses (~70% of his net worth)
- Real estate (~15% of his net worth)
- Other investments: he inherited about 15% of his net worth from family

When I asked him to provide specific advice for others on the path to wealth, he replied:

1. Work extremely hard.
2. Be intelligent.
3. Associate with the right people. ("Networking is the key," he added.)
4. Be optimistic and intuitive. ("My wife gets credit for this," he explained with a smile.)

In summary, Bobby utilized his education and hard work to be a successful employee and business consultant for many years. Much of his net worth was created through investable income and a one-time liquidity event from the sale of stock in the company his wife worked for. He then poured this investable income into a strong, diversified portfolio.

Building a substantial amount of wealth is great, but what you do with the money determines your level of greatness and fulfilment

TEN

From Worry to Wealth

At the beginning of this book, I made an audacious claim: Anyone can become wealthy. It is my hope that, by breaking down each variable and guiding you through the first three steps of wealth creation, I've given you the confidence to believe that statement and mobilize it in your own life. Wealth is truly accessible to everyone. No matter what your financial situation is, no matter what your goal is, and no matter what income and asset drivers you use to get there, a focused application of the wealth creation formula will get you there.

Let's recap the formula again:

Income (vA) *x* Assets (vB) *x* Leverage (vC) *x* Time (vD) = Wealth Creation

As we've clearly demonstrated throughout this book, this formula plays out differently for each person, and it can be endlessly tailored to an individual's unique circumstances.

One person may take on a student loan (vC) to get a master's degree and earn a high salary (vA), and then invest heavily in public securities (vB) to let them compound over time (vD).

Another person may begin selling mortgages on the side (vA) and partner with a contractor (vC) to invest in distressed properties (vB), rehabbing them to rent (vC) for long-term net worth gain (vD).

Another person may use their teaching experience and team up with a software developer (vC) to build an online tutoring business (vA, vB), ultimately selling it for $200k. Then they invest that $200k in a private equity fund (vB) and reinvest their earnings to compound to one million over time (vD).

Another person may downsize their home and car, generating them enough investable income (vA) to put a down payment down on a franchise (vB, vC), then grow that franchise to $300k. On the side they invest in public securities and acquire two rental properties, totaling a net worth of one million over time.

No matter how you look at it, everyone who becomes wealthy does so by using leverage to generate enough investable income to acquire assets that mature in value over time. Along the way, we can leverage those assets to generate more investable income to build us more debt-free assets. Throughout this process, we are using time not only to grow our assets over the long-term, but also as the essential resource that we are wisely investing every single day.

Remember, the goal of wealth building is to obtain financial freedom. Financial freedom comes when we no longer need to trade our active earning time for the money we need to cover our living expenses. But it doesn't have to be all or nothing; you don't have to wait until you're making $100k passively and then retire in one fell swoop. Even generating half of your necessary income from passive streams means you can scale back to working 2 or 3 days a week and begin investing that time into something that's more valuable to you.

My sister is a good example of this. She built up $75,000 by the age of 40, some of it from saving and some of it from the passing of a close relative.

Once she got there, she invested it in private mortgage lending, earning her an 8% return—$6,000 a year, or $500 a month.

At this point she could have taken that monthly $500 and bought a nicer car, house, vacation, etc., but instead she reinvested her earnings every year for 15 years. Because of compounding, she has built up an asset which now earns her $30,000 a year, or $2,500 a month.

Now, without touching the nest egg (the asset) itself, she can use that $2,500/month to pay her mortgage and car. She still works full time because she wants to, but by using the core principles of the wealth formula, she has significantly reduced her financial stress.

How can this work for you? Once you hit my recommended investable income target of $1,600/month, you can save $75,000 in 4 years. Then put your asset strategy to work, using leverage and time to grow that $75,000 into more income-producing assets. Depending on how soon you can reach $1,600/month in investable income, you could accomplish this within a decade.

I recognize that for many of you, getting to that $1,600/month target will not be easy. In order to solve your income and asset strategies, you will need to invest your time heavily up front into earning and learning. But now that you understand the science of wealth creation, I hope you can see that you simply need to get the snowball rolling. You won't need to work this hard forever. In fact, you will need to work harder over the course of your life, especially in your later years, if you *don't* start building assets that will eventually produce passive income!

So when *do* you retire? When do you get to take your foot off the gas?

That's entirely up to you! In my sister's case, she could keep reinvesting her $2,500/month and it would continue to grow, but she has chosen to start reaping the fruits of her sacrifice now. She also doesn't mind continuing to work full-time at this stage in her life. You may choose otherwise. You may choose to keep your investments growing longer and then retire completely once your nest egg is producing you $6,000/month. But the common denominator in all of these scenarios is that you get to choose! If you rely solely on active income for the remainder of your life, you don't get to choose. Either your health or social security will choose for you.

The Fundamentals

2020 was a painful reminder that, for most people, financial stress is either already tormenting us or it's just around the corner. Even people with strong salaries were suddenly panicking when the rug was pulled out from under them, because they had a low net worth. This is why I am very intentional about the financial targets that I recommend for people, because true financial stability is hard to achieve. Remember, both financial stability and financial freedom come from investing heavily in assets to grow your net worth.

Every week, people come to me asking different versions of the same question: *How can I solve my money problems?* And every week, I give different versions of the same answers. But even before I can discuss the principles of the wealth formula with them, together we have to check their foundation. Anyone with money problems can trace the source of their struggle back to a deficiency in at least one of four fundamental categories:

1. **Attitude**: Their mindset, beliefs, and motivations regarding money are misguided or lacking clarity.
2. **Behaviors**: Their daily and weekly use of time and money don't align with their goals.
3. **Knowledge**: They don't possess the right knowledge to earn income, acquire assets, and use leverage and time.
4. **Network**: They don't surround themselves with people that will help them learn and grow.

Let me be clear: You do not need money to become wealthy. But you do need the right attitude, behaviors, knowledge, and network.

Whether you are in the Worry stage and focusing on paying off high-interest debt, or in the Foundation stage and focusing on developing investable income, your *primary* focus should be on those four fundamentals. I said at the beginning of this book that the person you become is more important than the money you earn, and these four fundamentals are the way. They will help you earn more money and improve how you manage it. They will also help you make smarter investments as you grow from Foundation into the Stability, Growth, and Freedom stages.

We've discussed attitude time and again, but no amount of lecturing can cause it to spontaneously generate. No matter what your personality is, no matter what your background is, and no matter what struggles you face on a day-to-day basis, only you can change your attitude. Motivation, determination, honesty, diligence, and focus are all things you have to bring to the table. Without these, even the biggest bank account won't make you *feel* wealthy.

I hope that through this book you now truly *believe* that wealth is possible for you. My greatest wish is that you now have the faith and confidence that you can achieve your goals. You now know that, if you mix these ingredients and let it bake in the oven, you will get your "cake"—long-term wealth. Use this confidence in the results to motivate you to build healthy habits and strong discipline.

Someone who wakes up at 11am every day will never be wealthy. Someone who can't resist the temptation of an online advertisement will never be wealthy. Remember, time is our ultimate resource. What you think, do, and say every minute of every day produces what your life will become one week from now, one year from now, and twenty years from now. Cut out people and activities that waste your time. That alone will propel you forward in hugely important ways.

Instead, pour your time into learning and earning. Learn the specialized skills you need to increase your income. Learn more about different asset strategies and how to use leverage to multiply your money. If you follow the wealth formula—using income, time, and leverage to acquire more and more asset value—you *will* become wealthy. If you look at any self-made millionaire and examine how they used their time to learn and earn, you will find the same patterns. It *will* work for you if you follow the same pattern with the same diligence.

And lastly, remember that, after time, people are your most important asset. Your "network" means much more than just your professional connections. Who you surround yourself with plays an enormous role in your attitude, behaviors, and knowledge. Surround yourself with people who share your values and help you stay accountable to your goals. Seek out mentors to help you learn and grow. A good mentor is worth one hundred books. It is through connections with people that you can learn more skills, earn more income, leverage resources to acquire more assets, and become more aware of your own values and habits with money.

Just like with the four variables of the wealth formula or the five different selves of your being, these four fundamentals to success are all interdependent. Surround yourself with good people and your attitude improves. Learn more about personal growth and your behaviors improve, along with your mindset and network.

In all of this, building momentum is key. Get that snowball rolling downhill, no matter how small it may be. If you trip and your snowball gets lost in the trees, don't feel bad about yourself. Self-judgment will only hurt you. Dust yourself off, hit the reset button, revisit your goals, and go at it again.

From Worry to Wealth

All of this may seem easier said than done. Trust me, I understand. I grew up with a lot of financial pain. It wasn't that we couldn't put good food on our table or clothes on our backs. It was the fights, the stress, the anger, and the fear that financial insecurity caused that brought trauma to me and my family. As a result of this environment, my self-esteem was low, and I certainly didn't see myself as worthy of college or a well-paying job.

When you are in that position, it can be very difficult to believe there is another way. But it only takes meeting one person or reading one book to blow open the doors of curiosity and possibility. For me, it was meeting Terry Wilson and his recommendation to read *Think and Grow Rich*. He showed me that there was a different way that existed outside of what I knew from my family history. I recognized I was hurting, and that I needed to learn more.

The moment my beliefs about myself and the world around me changed, my behaviors, knowledge, and network changed too. Between the ages of 18 and 21, I went through a complete transformation, and it all stemmed from a burning desire to learn how to transcend the painful life that I had known. One action led to the next, and over the course of twenty years, my financial life unfolded. I didn't realize how it would play out at the time. No one does, but looking back years later, I can clearly see what positive actions led to my positive results.

I strongly believe that you have it in you to fulfill your desires and dreams. There is no other person like you. The very fact that you have read this book tells me that you have a fire within you that is craving to be fed. Make this book a catalyst to turn that fire into a raging inferno that will destroy your fears and negativity and push you towards your best financial self.

Seek out your "Terry Wilson" and start asking questions. The path to success and happiness in life is just asking one good question after another.

So go out there and get started—today.

If you're curious to learn more, visit **Yourjourney.WorrytoWealthBook.com** for tools, videos, courses, and coaching to help you discover your money values and align your behaviors to match those values and meet your goals. Use the coupon code *worrytowealth* to get 50% off the majority of Money Club courses.

Looking to build your network of positive financial influencers? Money Club's online community, Money Club, is a group of like-minded, like-hearted people who support each other in their quests to financial empowerment. Find out more at **wearemoneyclub.com**.

ACKNOWLEDGEMENTS

This book has been on my mind for many years. Many individuals influenced and inspired me to finally put my thoughts on paper, with the hope of helping others benefit from these ideas.

My wife Sherry Lyons has been my unwavering supporter throughout the ups and downs of my very colorful business path these past 37 years. Without her voice and encouragement, I may never have recovered from the low points of my journey. Along the way, my four kids—Taylor, Austin, Parker, and Jessica—have watched Dad focus on his goals and recognized the hard work it took to reach them. The four of you have given your dad a great deal of joy as I've watched each of you reach your own potential and best "self." Your dad is immensely proud of you!

My business partners, past and present, have all contributed to this book in their own incredibly special way.

To my partners at LYNK Capital—Alex Fink, Matt Brothers, Jarrod Ellis Beddingfield, and Dee-Toal Brothers—you guys have been great partners in our most recent journey, and I look forward to many more years growing the business together.

To my partners at Money Club—Aaron Velky, Josh Massey, and Gabe Bustos—your passion to help others learn and achieve financial intelligence and a better "self" is always inspiring. Your focus on building a community that allows all people to benefit from financial education is so critically important today. Keep building this awesome business!

To Ron Osher—because if you hadn't asked me to work for you 37 years ago, my life's course would not have been the same. For that, I sincerely need to thank you!

To my partner in Bavex Lending—Dave Goldstein—your work ethic and drive takes me back 30 years to when my career began, and I am inspired by what your future holds.

To Stewart Sachs—early on in my career you saw something in me that caused you to want to be my partner. I learned much from you about private lending and business in general, and my partnership with you proved extremely valuable to my knowledge and growth. I wish you continued success in your life's path.

There are many other successful entrepreneurs and associates that have given me advice and influence. These wonderful folks include Jay Dackman, esq., who for 25 years always supported my numerous business ventures and cheered me on from one idea to another.

An extra special acknowledgement is due to all the courageous people who stood by me through one of the lowest points of my career: when 6.1 million dollars was stolen from a bank escrow account that I had co-funded. Among those loyal friends was Alex Fink, who is still my business partner today. Despite also suffering great financial loss from this theft, he stuck by me and reminded me that I could build it back. He believed in me, and instead of parting ways after the ordeal, he encouraged me to drive forward and overcome this terrible event. Because of his encouragement, I followed his advice and grew my net worth far beyond what it had been. Alex, for your support during this tough time, I will be forever grateful.

To Paul Bekman, esq., who despite losing 1.25 million himself at the hands of a few bad people, remained faithful and encouraged me to fight forward and stay positive. Paul must be the most positive person I have ever met, and he has been one of my biggest cheerleaders for nearly 30 years. Paul, I am very grateful!

ABOUT THE AUTHOR

Ben Lyons is driven by the desire to help others transcend financial stress and worry in their lives. He began his career in 1983 immediately after graduating high school; by the age of 25, he owned 100 rental properties and a million-dollar lending business. Since then, he has been an initial investor and large shareholder of a commercial bank, a title company, a consumer finance company, and three mortgage banks. He has owned and managed over 375 residential and commercial real estate projects, and his lending organizations have produced more than 6.5 billion dollars in mortgages. Two of these organizations were ultimately sold to publicly traded insurance and financial organizations.

Widely considered an expert in private lending, Ben's true passion is empowering others with the knowledge of how to grow in and through the financial system. He published a book in 2016 titled *Be The Bank: Creating and Increasing*

Wealth Through Private Mortgage Lending, and has authored several white papers on the subject of lending and the utilization of leverage. He has been on the boards of three high schools and has been teaching financial literacy courses for over 20 years.

Currently, he serves as Founder, Managing Director, and Chief Credit Officer of the LYNK Capital Fund, a private equity firm based in Raleigh, North Carolina; Baltimore, Maryland; Charlotte, North Carolina; and Jacksonville, Florida. He is also the Wealth Strategist for Money Club.

Made in the USA
Columbia, SC
21 February 2023